THE STORY OF
THE ALEPH BETH

THE
STORY
OF
THE
ALEPH BETH

By

DAVID DIRINGER

THOMAS YOSELOFF
New York   London

Published 1960
Thomas Yoseloff, *Publisher*
11 East 36th Street
New York 16, N. Y.

Thomas Yoseloff Ltd.
123 New Bond Street
London W. 1, England

Library of Congress Catalog Card Number: 60-11321

Published under the joint sponsorship
of the World Jewish Congress

Printed in the United States of America

CONTENTS

PART II

EARLY HEBREW ALPHABET

6

7

LIST OF PLATES

PREFACE

THE PURPOSE OF the present book, which has been written at the invitation of the World Jewish Congress—British Section, is to provide a general introduction to the history of the Hebrew alphabet. I have endeavored to present the main facts about this alphabet and its background, in moderate compass and without much technicality, to avoid, however, the form of a literary essay or a philosophical treatise, or even of an exposition of the scientific palaeographic view-point. It has been my aim to show that the Hebrew alphabet is both one of the World's most original discoveries and the result of a long intellectual evolution.

In a popular book like this, written mainly for "the man in the street", there is little point, even if it were practicable, to deal in detail with the slow evolution of the single letters throughout the ages and in the various countries of the East and West. It seemed desirable to devote more space to generally less-known problems, to the origins of the two main Hebrew scripts, to the connection between them and other systems, and to the historical background. In the last thirty years, the history of the Alphabet, or what in America is now called "Alphabetology", has been receiving more attention, after decades of neglect. This is no doubt due, in part, to important archaeological discoveries, particularly in the Holy Land and the neighboring countries, which have added much to our understanding of the origins and early development of the Alphabet in general and the Early Hebrew alphabet in particular. But although literature on certain aspects of, and problems connected with, the Hebrew alphabet has thus been increasing in volume it does not appear that any attempt has been made to treat the subject as a whole.

For practical reasons no attempt has been made to give an exhaustive account of all the pertinent material—more especially the material which more properly belongs to the domain of Hebrew palaeography; and documentation has been restricted to a minimum. Even so, were it not for the assistance of the Cultural Department of the World Jewish Congress (headed by Dr A. Steinberg) and the World Jewish Congress—

11

British Section (with Dr S. Roth as its General Secretary) this book could not have been published at such a popular price. I tender my sincere gratitude to Mrs and Mr L. A. Freeman, and to Mr D. J. Trenner, the indefatigable Secretary of the Cultural Committee of the World Jewish Congress—British Section, who have read my text in typescript and made valuable criticisms and suggestions in detail.

University of Cambridge   D.D.

INTRODUCTION

I HAVE TRAVELLED a bit and encountered quite a lot of illiteracy: in Europe, in Africa and in Asia. The very descendants of the once most civilized nations in the World, the Mesopotamians, the Egyptians, and other now Arabian nations, the Greeks, the Italians (in the South and on the main islands), the Spaniards: all show a high proportion of illiteracy. But I have hardly found a Jew who does not know at least how to read his prayers.

Half a century ago, in Eastern Europe, Jews learned at school to read and write three different languages with different scripts; at home they spoke another quite different language with a distinct script, and in the Cheder they learned the Sacred Scriptures in yet another language and script.

It would be wrong to assume that the average Jew ever mastered all these languages, but he could make himself understood in most of them, and to a varying degree could write them. I am, indeed, fortunate that I still remember something of what I was supposed to learn half a century ago.

When I grew older—though my situation became worse and worse—I became more interested in the origins of the various scripts I then came to know, and I was told that the origin of the Hebrew alphabet was quite simple: *aleph* derived from the form of an ox's head, *beth* from the form of a house, *gimel* from the form of a camel, and so on. I was content with that!

Thirty years later I realized how little I knew: the *A–B–C* is not as easy as we had been made to believe, but its origin and its story are so fascinating and of such interest for our study of civilized mankind that I for one made up my mind to dedicate to this problem many years of study. In the present treatise, the necessity for brevity (imposed by the publisher) and simplicity (this book being intended for "the man in the street") may lead to false impressions. Indeed, it may be presumptuous to attempt so brief a survey of so vast a field. Yet, it is to be hoped that the chief purpose may in some measure be served, no matter what the faults may be.

*   *   *

13

When one is faced with a cardinal historical problem such as the "origin of the alphabet", inquiry into first causes is extraordinarily difficult. The late Italo-American Prof. Chiera has rightly pointed out that there never was a man who could sit down and say, "Now I am going to be the first man to write". Writing, that supreme achievement of man, the one which makes possible the very existence of civilization by transmitting to later generations the acquisitions of their predecessors, was the result of a slow and natural development. Even with recent events of any magnitude, it is difficult to determine their precise origin: indeed, in trying to trace them back to their source, we reach a stage where cause and effect condition each other and follow each other in turn. To avoid this conundrum we must, so to speak, choose a starting point, a birth certificate.

A birth certificate may, indeed, be found for several alphabets, but it is not easy to find it for the Hebrew script. The main difficulty lies in the fact that the decisive factor is not the external form, the shape of the individual letters, but the phonetic or sound value of the symbols. For the origin of the Hebrew alphabet, therefore, we need to go back to the origin of the early North-Semitic alphabet as used, fully-developed, in inscriptions in the last centuries of the second millennium B.C.E. The alphabet of these inscriptions contains the same number of letters, in the same order, and having the same phonetic values as in the Hebrew alphabet used in the days of David and Solomon or in the Hebrew alphabet as used at present. It is unique. The case of the Greek or Latin, of the Russian or Arabic, or of any other alphabetic script, is totally different. Their history is full of change, involving the elimination or addition of symbols, changes in pronunciation, the combination of two or more symbols to represent single sounds, and so on.

(Hence, it would seem appropriate that a story of the Hebrew alphabet should start with the origin of the North-Semitic alphabet, and indeed with the origin of The Alphabet.)

*   *   *

Recently, I was privileged to hear a lecture on Biblical Archaeology by a leading excavator, Sir Leonard Woolley; in his view, Palestine, as compared with Mesopotamia, for instance, is not worth excavating. Many archaeologists who

14

were present would not, I think, have agreed with him. Be that as it may, there is one field of archaeology in which the Holy Land is infinitely superior to all other ancient centers of civilization—that bearing on the origin of the Alphabet. (All evidence at present available seems to suggest that the region of the Holy Land gave birth to the Alphabet.)

*   *   *

The intricate problems bearing on the origin of the Alphabet and its pre-history, as well as the general history of the Alphabet in all ages and lands, are the contents of PART I, which deals with The Background of the Hebrew alphabet.

PART II examines the thousand-year-long development of the Early Hebrew alphabet (also known as the "Phoenician-Hebrew" or "Old Hebrew"), which was the script of the ancient Israelites, of their kings and prophets, of the chancelleries of the United Kingdom of Israel and of the kingdoms of Israel and Judah.

PART III, partly overlapping with Part II, deals with the development of the Square Hebrew alphabet, ancestor of the modern Hebrew scripts. Square Hebrew (though partly influenced by the Early Hebrew) derived from the Aramaic alphabet, which already had a long history, of nearly one thousand years. For about 500 years the Jews knew, and to some extent used, the Aramaic alphabet. In the post-exilic period, both the Early Hebrew and the Aramaic alphabets were employed concurrently for several centuries. However, in the third to second centuries B.C.E. the consonantal Square Hebrew alphabet became standardized. From then on, in its bi-millennial history, the Square Hebrew alphabet can be distinguished in two periods of approximately a thousand years each: (a) the period of consolidation; this includes the creation of the systems of vocalization and standardization of the Tiberian system of "punctuation" (see Chapters 1–3 of Part III); (b) the period of standardized use, with only very slight and purely technical changes in the shapes of the letters, due mainly to the writing materials and tools employed and to the necessity of speed on the one hand, and of readability on the other; this is dealt with in Part III, Chapters 4 and 5.

In the Conclusion, we examine the problem of the reform of the Hebrew alphabet, a problem which comes to the fore from time to time.

15

PART I

THE BACKGROUND
Pl. I–II

CHAPTER 1

i. IMPORTANCE OF WRITING

THE INVENTION OF WRITING must rank among the great landmarks of human culture. It is so fundamental that one is astonished that it appeared so late in the development of mankind. While man's creative and destructive powers have been developing for an incalculable number of years, the spiritual and intellectual progress of mankind became marked only at a very late stage. In man's spiritual advance, writing holds a place second only to that of speech, as an essential means of communication within society. There is no people on earth without language, this being a natural distinction of mankind. Writing, even more peculiar to man than speech, is in some sense a refinement of speech.

WRITING AND CIVILIZATION

In the opinion of some thinkers (Kant, Mirabeau, Carlyle, and others), the invention of writing was the real beginning of civilization. The anthropologists W. Schmidt and W. Koppers divided man's spiritual growth into the period before he could write and the period after he learnt to write. J. H. Breasted considered writing of greater importance in uplifting the human race than any other intellectual achievement. H. Frankfort makes writing the crucial test of civilization.

According to V. Gordon Childe the main elements of ancient civilizations were: specialization, effective concentration of economic and political power, writing, and conventional standards of weights and measures leading to some mathematical and calendrical science. In Sir Leonard Woolley's opinion, organized and durable administration would be a precarious thing if it lacked the transmitting of experience and the intellectual heredity that writing alone secures: writing is not a secondary consequence of civic life, but a condition of it. And finally, Sir Mortimer Wheeler agrees with Sir Leonard that the term "civilization", in its fullest sense, implies some measure of literacy.

19

Further, we can hardly imagine the complex society of a higher civilization with its highly developed science and technology, and particularly with its literature and newspapers, without the art of writing. If some recent writers have decried writing as an instrument by which cliques of priests and rulers have enslaved the far more useful manual workers, the very injustice was surely brought to our attention by these authors by means of writing.

WRITING VERSUS TRADITION

The first and perhaps the most obvious advantage is that writing gives permanence to man's knowledge. Without letters, there can be no permanent knowledge. Unable to write, pre-historic man expressed his soul by means of the spoken word with the aid of gesture and song. The lore once acquired, the *pater familias* or story-tellers passed it on, by word of mouth, to the children, and lived with other oral traditions in their memories. Indeed, story-telling was one of the oldest cultural manifestations of man. We know, for instance, that Polynesian story-tellers trained their own memories and that of their sons so that they were able to hand down to posterity by word of mouth their people's history and especially their valuable migration traditions. The oral tradition and the mythology thus shaped and preserved by the minds of those primitive peoples—of the distant or of the more recent past—is an ocean filled with pearls, but it is far from sufficient for the reconstruction of the life of those peoples. To record real history, we require something very different; we require actual and reliable record; at the very least, we require contemporary written documents.

INVENTION OF WRITING ASCRIBED TO GODS OR MYTHICAL CHARACTERS

In short, writing—this most important system of human communication by means of conventional symbols—is an integral part of our civilization. We do not know who the inventor was: there were probably many inventors; nor do we know when or where the knowledge of the art first arose: it probably came to be known in the dim and distant past; perishable writing materials (such as bark, wood and leaves) were used for the purpose. The tradition of the invention had already been lost in very ancient times. The Bible deals with the origin of various arts, such as language—the Tower of Babel; agriculture—*Gen.* ii. 15; iv. 2; xxvi. 12; *Isaiah* xxviii. 26, etc.; music—*Gen.* iv. 20–22, and numerous other passages; metallurgy—in *Gen.* iv. 22 we are told that Tubalcain was "an instructor of every artificer in brass and iron", and so on. But in the whole Bible there is no reference to the origin of writing, though there is a post-Biblical tradition which attributes the creation of writing to Moses.

It is only too obvious that because of the great value set upon writing and the magical power it exercises over the unlearned, this precious possession of man was regarded as something beyond his unaided powers of creation. The ancient Egyptians ascribed the invention to Thoth, the god who invented nearly all the cultural elements, or to the goddess Isis; the Babylonian tradition attributed it to Nebo, Marduk's son, who was also the god of man's destiny, or to Namar-Bili; the ancient Chinese to the dragon-faced Ts'ang Chien; the ancient Greeks to Hermes, or to various other mythical characters, particularly to Kadmos; the Romans attributed the invention to their god Mercury. The Teuton god Odin or Wotan was credited with the invention of the Runes and the Celtic god Ogmios with the invention of the Oghams; even in pre-Columbian America, in Mexico, the Aztecs attributed their writing to their God Quetzalcoatl. The Indians and many other peoples also believed in the divine origin of the script.

ii. PRODROMES OF WRITING

From the earliest times, we can detect various parallel efforts to develop methods of human communication. Language led to the development of acoustic methods. Instances are the news-cries of the Veddas of Ceylon, of the Central African Pygmies, of the Negritos of N. Luzon; the scalp-cries of the N. American Hurons and Iroquois, the whooping-communications of the N. American Creek Indians. The range of the human voice was extended by signalling with drums, in W. Africa, S. America, New Guinea, and elsewhere, with horns or trumpets in the Cameroons, S. America, Caroline Islands, with flutes in the N. Cameroons, E. Sudan, and by similar means elsewhere. Of these, the most common was, and still is, the signalling drum, known as tom-tom, which makes possible the development of complete code systems of endless possibilities.

VISUAL METHODS OF COMMUNICATION

Acoustic methods of communication are allied with the optic or visual methods, such as gesture, mimicry, lip reading, but particularly those employing light, fire, smoke (N. American and S. American Indians, Eskimos, W. African tribes; Morse Code; systems used by seamen, scouts, and others). Signalling indicating S.O.S. messages often received lasting quality by means of road- or trail-signs, sign poles, heaps of stones, signal posts, etc., as warning signals, appeals for help, notched sticks planted along the trail indicating the direction of a stricken camp, and so on.

PROPERTY MARKS

Property marks, very common among many peoples, are announcements to the public that a certain object belongs to a certain person or group of persons; here we may refer to the *wusums* or cattle-marks of Arab tribes, to the *tamgas* or symbolical marks or seals of early Turki tribes; to the canoe-marks of the Eskimos; to the reindeer-marks of the Lapps, of the Tungus cut in the ears of the animals or of Samoyeds burned in the thighs of the animals. We may also refer to tattooing and similar distinguishing marks, to the medieval and modern heraldic signs, including coat-armor, pennons, and so on, and to the modern trade-marks. Pottery marks were used in pre-dynastic and early dynastic Egypt (late 4th mill. and early 3rd mill. B.C.E.) as well as in ancient Palestine, Crete, Cyprus, and in the whole Mediterranean area some centuries later.

MEMORY-AID DEVICES

By setting up a monument on a grave, a person intends to perpetuate the memory of the deceased. Many examples of stone-pillars as memory-aid devices can be quoted from the Bible. Instances are *Gen.* xxxi. 48, *Josh.* xxii. 26–27 and

xxiv. 26–27. Of universal nature are the memory-aids of the notched sticks and the knotted cord; there are the carved message-sticks of the primitive Australians, which served intertribal affairs; the notched sticks of ancient Scandinavia, used to help in conveying messages or in spreading important news such as a state of war or the convoking of an assembly; the carved sticks trimmed with feathers which the Lutsu (E. Tibet) used for declaration of war; the notched sticks used in ancient Russia, Italy, North America, etc., and still used in Africa, China, Australia and elsewhere. Notched sticks, or *tallies*, were actually used by the Exchequer of England down to 1832, as receipts for money paid into the Treasury.

Finally, we may refer to the churingas of the Australian aborigines, which are sacred stones covered with crystal markings, used as notations or memory-aids for recounting the traditional myths of the origin of the tribe. They are handed to boys at their initiation.

One of the commonest devices to recall to mind something to be done is, of course, to tie a knot in a handkerchief; the Catholic rosary—each bead of which, according to position and size, is supposed to recall a certain prayer—is a similar memory-aid device.

Of the knot devices—which were employed in ancient Tibet, Japan, Bengal, Persia and Mexico, and are still used in E. Africa, Polynesia, Peru, and many other places—the most famous is the *quipu* (or the knotted cord) found in the ancient graves of Peru, which were used mainly to "write down" administrative facts, to register the amount of taxes, etc., by means of strings and knots of varied length, thickness and color; it would also seem that poems and literary works were transcribed in such *quipu*.

COMMUNICATION BY MEANS OF TANGIBLE OBJECTS

Cara tribes (Ecuador) put pebbles of different shape, color and size into small wooden boxes to record numbers or events; the Iroquois (N. America) *wampum*-belts, which consisted of cords of colored shell-bead occasionally arranged in pictorial drawings, served as legal instruments in concluding a contract; white stood for peace, red for war or anger, black for death or misfortune, yellow for gold or tribute, etc. The *calumet*, or

23

sacred decorated reed tobacco pipe, was another N. American memory-aid device; it was used for signifying war or peace.

Means of communication with the help of tangible objects are unlimited. A girl in E. Turkestan sent to her boy friend a "love-letter" consisting of a small bag, containing a lump of pressed tea ("I can drink tea no more"), a blade of straw ("because I became sickly for love of you"), a dried-up apricot ("I became shrivelled-up"), a red fruit ("I become red when I think of you"), a piece of charcoal ("my heart burns of love"), a feather of a falcon ("if I had wings I would fly to you"), a flower ("you are handsome"), a piece of sugar candy ("you are sweet"), and a pebble ("but is your heart made of stone?").

A Yoruba man (Nigeria), taken prisoner by a king of Dahomey, sent a message to his wife consisting of a stone ("my body is healthy, hard like a stone"), a piece of coal ("but my prospects are dark, black like coal"), some pepper ("and my mind is heated"), some corn ("I have become thin") and a rag ("my clothes are worn and torn"). Among the Lutsu in E. Tibet, a piece of chicken liver, three pieces of chicken fat, and a chili, wrapped in red paper, indicated the warning "prepare to fight at once".

Most interesting were the symbolical *aroko* ("to convey news") of the Yebu and other tribes in Nigeria; the *aroko* consisted of cowries (small shells), two strung back to back being a message of reproof for non-payment of debts, six meaning "attracted", eight meaning "agreed", etc.

Finally, the Greek historian Herodotus (iv. 131 ff.) mentions a "letter" which the Scythians, ancient inhabitants of Southern Russia, sent to the Persian king Darius; it consisted of a bird, a mouse, a frog, and five arrows. The Persians gave various interpretations of this message, the best one was supposed to mean "Persians, can you fly like a bird into the sky, hide yourself in the ground like a mouse, leap through swamps like a frog? Otherwise, do not try to go to war with us: we shall overwhelm you with arrows."

PICTOGRAPHY

It was a great step forward when instead of using tangible objects, Man began to "write" (to scratch, to draw, to paint, to incise) pictures of things and at a second stage to "write" picture stories, that is, to draw a series of pictures which "speak" for themselves, so as to tell a connected story, to set forth an epic or a song. Such "writings" are found everywhere, but they can best be studied amongst some native tribes of North and Central America, of Western Africa, of Polynesia and Australia, and amongst the Yukaghirs of N.E. Siberia. Most famed are the chronicles or winter-counts of the Dakotas of N. America; another well-known pictorial document is the *walam olum* ("true-to-life" painting) of the history of the Delaware Indians. There are the pictorial drawings and paintings of the Eskimos and other arctic tribes, of the Prairie Indians, which are in effect records with "descriptions" of everyday occurrences, of special events and of tribal traditions. All these and many other primitive devices of communication —which are based on the human necessity of social intercourse, the needs of trading, and particularly the needs of religion and magic—are prodromes of writing or embryo-writing, none constituting a complete system. Such devices are doubtless as old as any human community.

SYMPATHETIC MAGIC

The oldest extant are the devices connected with magic, known as "sympathetic magic". The world of primitive man was and is a world of magic. Among the oldest forms of magic are those dealing with procuring food. In some remote period, in the Upper Old Stone Age, belonging perhaps to 20,000 B.C.E., Primitive Man, the cave-dweller in S. France and N.E. Spain, drew sketches of his prey—bears, buffaloes, deer, and other animals—on the wall of his cave, and painted them with colored earths and vegetable dyes. He also sketched on the bones of the animals he killed, and on rude stone implements. Some of these reproductions were remarkable for their realism. In the mind of Prehistoric Man, the picture of the prey was in some way identified with the living animal. When he pierced the image with his spear, in his mind the success of the coming hunt was assured. To this day, Australian natives substitute sand-drawings of the prey for the prehistoric ochre-painting.

Probably to be included in the category of "sympathetic magic" are the various geometric signs or conventional figures of men, painted or engraved on stones, termed "petroglyphs", of megalithic tombs (New Stone Age), and the like, found in

CHAPTER 2

DEVELOPMENT OF WRITING

WE CANNOT KNOW all the links in the chain of development of writing from the rude beginnings as described in the previous chapter down to the fully evolved alphabetic script. Difficulties also arise when we try to fix in detail the stages of this development, to find exact terms for these various stages, to define them, and to ascribe to them the individual scripts. We have attempted to distinguish four or five main groups of scripts below, but must point out that some of the scripts we assign to class (i) have features of class (ii) or (iii), whereas other scripts also assigned to (i) may be regarded as transitional from "embryo-writing" to (iii). The Maya and Aztec scripts, of ancient Central America and Mexico, and, though probably less so, the mysterious Easter Island script, are cases in point.

STAGES OF DEVELOPMENT OF WRITING

The successive stages of "writing" may be indicated in this schematic way:

(i) *Iconography*, which consists of drawings of natural objects. These drawings are disconnected and fragmentary pictures which give a static impression, as compared with:

(ii) *Synthetic or Ideographic Writing*, which consists of a series of pictures telling connected stories.

Both these stages have already been referred to in the previous chapter.

MAIN SCRIPTS OF ANCIENT WORLD

(iii) The most famous scripts of the ancient world, those of the Mesopotamian peoples, the Egyptians, the Cretans (also known as Minoans), the Indus Valley script, the Hittite hieroglyphics, the Chinese, the Maya and Aztec scripts, the Easter Island script, and certain minor systems, are more or less complete systems of writing.

They are generally, but incorrectly, called "ideographic". Some of them may, indeed, have been ideographic in origin, but even in the earliest inscriptions which have come to light, the scripts are partly ideographic—using pictographic symbols which suggest ideas or represent objects—and partly phonetic, the components being combined in various ways. The term "pictographic" for "ideographic" is even less appropriate.

(Another term for these systems of writing is "transitional", these scripts representing the transitional stage between pure ideographic writing and the pure phonetic system (see below). A still better term would be "analytic")

In these various systems, a standardized picture, a pictogram, which was usually easily reproduced and familiar to those using it, was selected by convention from the many which had been used for the particular thing, and became the accepted symbol of its name. The name of the object, whether at rest or in some particular form of motion, was closely identified with the picture, at least originally. Associated with pictograms were signs of a different type, known as ideograms, which represented ideas, qualities, actions, and sometimes objects, none of which could be clearly portrayed by a pictogram.

The Chinese is the only system belonging to this group which is still in use.

Each of these systems presents sufficient problems to fill a book by itself. Here we can only refer to a few important examples. The Egyptian writing, in use for over 3,500 years (from c. 3000 B.C.E. to the sixth century C.E.) had three varieties: the monumental hieroglyphic, in which the symbols always maintained their pictorial character; the hieratic, a cursive form used mainly as a literary hand; and the demotic script, a still more cursive form which originated in the 7th century B.C.E., and was mainly used for commercial and private purposes. Mesopotamian writing underwent considerable change as it passed from the Sumerians into the hands of the Akkadians (Babylonians and Assyrians), the Hurrians, the Hittites, the Persians, and other peoples. This script is generally known as "cuneiform", because it came to be written by pressing little wedge-shaped marks into clay. The symbols soon lost any resemblance to the objects they were originally supposed to represent.

Early in the period of the Old Kingdom, that is during the

third millennium B.C.E., the Egyptian writing had come to include 24 signs which stood for separate uni-consonantal words, thus constituting a sort of alphabetic system within the larger body of bi-consonantal and tri-consonantal symbols. The Egyptians, however, did not recognize the great value of this invention if used independently, and clung to their cumbersome mixed system. On the other hand, the Assyrians succeeded in simplifying the whole cuneiform system, and at a later stage the Assyrian cuneiform script practically became a syllabic script, in which each sign denoted a syllable; the number of wedges used in the individual sign was reduced and the writing became more square in appearance.

PHONETIC SYSTEMS OF WRITING

(iv) In the "embryo-writings" and in pure ideography, the symbols can be "read" in any language: there is no necessary connection between the depicted symbol and the recorded speech, with the result that we can examine and appreciate the pictorial and ideographic signs of any people who have ever existed, without knowing what words they spoke. On the other hand, in phonetic systems, writing has become the graphic counterpart of speech. Each element of writing corresponds to a specific element of speech, a sound, in the language to be represented, and the symbols cease to be self-interpreting pictures. The individual signs may be of any shape; generally there is no connection between the external form of the symbol and the sound it represents and the script must be explained through the language in which it is written.

SYLLABIC SYSTEMS

Phonetic systems may be syllabic or alphabetic. In the systematic syllabaries, the individual signs represent syllables: these units are the smallest elements of words that can be isolated and spoken. Thus, as the written symbols (phonograms) of a syllabary are monosyllabic in value, a word of one syllable would, of course, be represented by one symbol, whereas a word of two or more syllables would be represented by a group of two or more symbols or phonograms. The syllabic systems developed more easily and appeared as new creations more often than did an alphabet.

29

In the case of a language that, for whatever reason, has many clusters of consonants, the syllabary would become a cumbrous mode of writing, especially because it generally contains only open syllables (that is, those made up of consonant plus vowel) or vowels when these constitute syllables. This is particularly noticeable in the ancient Cypriot syllabary, in which the Greek word *ptolin* ("city") was transliterated *po-to-li-ne*. Thus, while it would be easy to write a word like "de-fi-ni-te", the word "sprinkle", for instance, would have to be written something like "si-pi-ri-ne-ke-le", and such a representation of sounds would certainly require a much greater number of symbols than in alphabetic writing.

Some syllabic scripts have already been referred to: the late Assyrian script, the Japanese (of which there are two varieties, *Hiragana* and *Katakana*, both evolved in ancient times from the Chinese script) and the ancient Cypriot scripts (probably derived from the Minoan). Another ancient syllabary was employed at Byblos (N. Syria), whereas artificial modern syllabaries existed or still exist in W. Africa, N. America, China, and in a few other regions.

Two scripts—"poor half and half things" derived from more complicated scripts, without reaching true simplicity—almost reached the stage of becoming alphabets. One was the historically very important Early Persian script, the official script of the Achaemenid dynasty, under whose rule, from the mid-sixth century B.C.E. until the victories of Alexander the Great, the Persians became the most important power in the then known world. The other was the Meroïtic script, used in two varieties (monumental and cursive) from the second century B.C.E. to the fourth century C.E. in the kingdom of Meroë, the ancient Nubia. While the Early Persian cuneiform script was a mixture of alphabetic and syllabic symbols, the Meroïtic contained only two syllabic signs, all the other symbols being alphabetic.

THE ALPHABET

(v) So we come to alphabetic writing, which we may fairly regard as in principle the finished product of all this long train of development. Indeed, the stage of alphabetic writing is the last, the most highly developed, the most convenient form, and it is readily adaptable to almost any language. It is a collection

30

of a small number of symbols, generally between 20 and 30, known as letters, intended to represent the various elementary sounds used by the human voice in speech.

Alphabetic writing is now universally employed by civilized peoples; no other system of writing has had so extensive, so intricate, and so interesting a history. It is now generally agreed that all existing alphabets, and those no longer used, derived from one original alphabet. In its broad lines, the story of the alphabet since the end of the second millennium B.C.E. is not very hard to trace, but many details of its origin and of the origin of some individual alphabets are still uncertain.

CHAPTER 3

CREATION OF THE ALPHABET

NEARLY TWENTY YEARS ago, the leading American Orientalist, Prof. W. F. Albright, remarked that one of the most encouraging aspects of Syro-Palestinian archaeology today is the speed with which old problems are being solved and new ones introduced and brought into the foreground. This statement aptly describes the problem of origin of the Alphabet, and its early development. The problem of the date of invention of the Alphabet, it would seem, has been partly solved: no serious scholar now disagrees with the theory that the Alphabet originated at least as early as about the middle of the second millennium B.C.E. It is also generally agreed that the Alphabet was created or, at any rate, became standardized, in the region of Syria-Palestine; that the N. Semitic alphabet became the ancestor of the Greek (the prototype of all the European alphabets), of the Central Asiatic and the Indian alphabets, and so on.

The new problems which are still unsolved are: the exact position of the Palaeo-Sinaitic script, the Early Canaanite alphabet, the pseudo-hieroglyphic Byblos inscriptions, the Ugarit cuneiform alphabet, etc. *vis-à-vis* the N. Semitic alphabet. While the majority of scholars take the view that cuneiform writing and some other ancient scripts did not exercise a decisive influence on the formation of the Alphabet, it is widely held that the Egyptian hieroglyphic script had some influence, though there is still disagreement as to its extent. In short, the main problem still awaits solution.

THEORIES CONCERNING THE ORIGIN OF THE ALPHABET

Over the centuries, various theories have been advanced by scholars to explain the origin of alphabetic writing. The Egyptian, the cuneiform, the Cretan, and other scripts, have been proposed as the prototypes of alphabetic writing. Sir W. M. Flinders Petrie argued that the Greek and the Phoenician alphabets, and other early alphabetic and non-alphabetic scripts developed from the geometric prehistoric marks employed throughout the Mediterranean region from the earliest times. According to him, the first system of classification originated in N. Syria; "daughter" systems were developed by adding some signs and omitting others. Dr. T. H. Gaster at one time revised this prehistoric-geometric-signs theory.

Since 1916, the Palaeo-Sinaitic theory has been much in favor: this theory was advanced particularly by Dr. (now Sir) Alan Gardiner. It is based on inscriptions discovered by W. M. Flinders Petrie in the Sinaitic Peninsula in 1905. Dr. Gardiner and Prof. Kurt Sethe, dealing with these inscriptions came to the conclusion that they represent a stage of writing intermediate between Egyptian hieroglyphics and the N. Semitic alphabet. The date of these inscriptions is disputed, some scholars attributing them to the early eighteenth century B.C.E., and others, with more probability, to the fifteenth century. Although this theory has been accepted by many leading scholars, it cannot be said to have been conclusively proved. Accordingly, for chronological and other reasons, the Palaeo-Sinaitic script cannot yet be regarded as the great mother-alphabet of all the alphabetic scripts.

Bible scholars have been trying to find a connection between the Palaeo-Sinaitic script and the Biblical references to the earliest "writings" attributed to Moses at Sinai, but have been unable to do so.

EARLY CANAANITE INSCRIPTIONS
Pl. I

The solution of the problem of origin of the Alphabet may come from Palestine, where since 1929 several Middle and Late Bronze inscriptions have been discovered. These inscriptions can be divided into three groups, belonging to (1) the eighteenth or seventeenth century B.C.E.; (2) the fifteenth or fourteenth century; and (3) the thirteenth century B.C.E. For readers with an interest in curious facts, may I draw attention to the fact that, probably by sheer coincidence, the three groups correspond roughly to three notable periods: the first, to the Age of the Patriarchs (eighteenth to sixteenth century B.C.E.); the second, to the age of Joshua (fourteenth century); the third,

33

to the Age of the Judges (second half of the thirteenth century B.C.E.); the gap of two to three centuries between the first and the second groups corresponds roughly to the period of oppression of the Israelites in Egypt. At any rate, it is now evident that alphabet writing was employed in Canaan and neighboring districts from the time of the Patriarchs.

OTHER ALPHABETIC ATTEMPTS

Leading scholars have agreed that alphabet-making was at that time in the air and that the Early Canaanite system (or systems) suggests that that country was a main center of experiments aiming at the invention of the Alphabet.

Other attempts seem to have been made in neighboring countries. For example, since 1929 several bronze or stone inscriptions of the second millennium B.C.E. have been discovered at Byblos, in N. Syria, incised or engraved in a hitherto unknown pseudo-hieroglyphic script. An enigmatic inscription, of the early twelfth century B.C.E., was discovered in 1931 at Balu'a, Biblical Moab, in Transjordan. Another attempt at alphabetic writing is apparently revealed by inscriptions in prehistoric geometric signs of the second millennium B.C.E., discovered in various Egyptian sites by Sir W. M. Flinders Petrie. Other still undeciphered inscriptions written, it would seem, in tentative alphabetic scripts have been found at Ur of the Chaldees, the home of the Patriarch Abraham, in Syria, and in Asia Minor.

UGARITIC CUNEIFORM ALPHABET

Finally, reference must be made to the Ugarit and the South Semitic alphabets, two early fully developed systems of alphabetic writing. An epoch-making discovery was made in 1929 and the succeeding years at the ancient Ugarit, on the Syrian coast opposite the most easterly cape of Cyprus, following the accidental find in 1928 of a subterranean tunnel in the village of Râs Shamrah. Thousands of clay-tablets, documents of inestimable value in many fields of research, such as epigraphy, philology, the history of religion, were found, written in a hitherto unknown cuneiform-alphabet of 30 letters, which was soon deciphered. A few texts belong to the 15th century B.C.E., but it is difficult to fix the date of origin of the script. The use

34

of this writing seems to have ceased in the 13th century, although we have evidence only for the 14th.

Among the theories on the problem of origin of this script, the most natural one is that it was invented by a native who knew the N. Semitic alphabet, but was accustomed to the use of clay and stylus, the standard materials used for cuneiform writing, but which were not suitable for writing linear letters. From the N. Semitic alphabet he borrowed the idea of an alphabetic consonantal writing; from cuneiform writing he imitated the wedge-shaped elements, which he arranged in various simple combinations. This opinion seems to be confirmed by the discovery in Ugarit in 1949 of a 14th-century small tablet containing the oldest known *ABC*, in which the thirty Ugarit letters are so placed that the 22 phonemes which are the same as in the N. Semitic alphabet appear in exactly the same order. Of the additional letters, three were later additions and were added at the end of the *ABC*; also, there were three *alephs* representing the sounds of *a, i, u,* instead of one in the N. Semitic alphabet.

SOUTH-SEMITIC ALPHABETS

The problem of origin of the S. Semitic alphabets is more complicated. This important branch, which was used in Arabia from the late second millennium B.C.E. down to Islamic times, had an offshoot in Africa, the Ethiopic alphabet, the ancestor of the modern Amharic, Tigré, Tigriña, and other alphabets still in use.

There is no doubt that the two main branches (the N. Semitic and the S. Semitic) are interconnected, but what exactly the degree of contact was cannot, as yet, be determined.

NORTH-SEMITIC ALPHABETS

Until a generation ago, very few ancient inscriptions had been found in Syria and Palestine written in a local script. The earliest datable known example of the N. Semitic alphabet was the Moabite Stone or Mesha' stele (cf. 2 *Kings,* iii. 4–5), dating from about the middle of the ninth century B.C.E. This inscription constituted the starting point for the study of the Alphabet.

A new chapter in the history of writing began in 1923 with

the discovery at Byblos of the Aḥiram sarcophagus, containing a N. Semitic inscription in two lines. It is now generally attributed to the eleventh century B.C.E. More recently several somewhat earlier inscriptions have been found at Byblos. These inscriptions and a few others which come either from Syria or from Palestine—such as the Gezer Calendar, attributed to *c.* 1000 B.C.E.: see further on—may be considered a trustworthy starting-point for the history of the Alphabet.

The script of these inscriptions shows close external resemblances even in detail with that of Early Hebrew, Phoenician and Aramaic documents of the first millennium B.C.E. Moreover, several letters in the Aḥiram sarcophagus (*aleph, waw, ṭeth, yodh, nun, 'ayin, pe* and *resh*) indicate a cursive rather than a monumental development: one gets the impression that the stone-cutter copied this inscription from a text written on papyrus. The phonetic value of a few letters (particularly of *samekh* and *shin*) suggests that some letters may have dropped out even earlier and others amalgamated with the existing ones. Thus, both internal and external evidence suggest that the N. Semitic alphabet originated several centuries earlier than these inscriptions.

This proposition is supported by the Ugarit alphabet, referred to above, which presupposes the existence of the N. Semitic alphabet about the middle of the second millennium B.C.E. It is thus possible that the N. Semitic alphabet, or a direct predecessor of it, a Proto-Semitic alphabet, originated in the eighteenth or the seventeenth century B.C.E. It may have been the Early Canaanite script, already referred to, or a parallel script. It may have been the ancestor of the Palaeo-Sinaitic script and of the South-Semitic alphabets.

WHEN, BY WHOM, AND WHERE WAS THE ALPHABET INVENTED?

We may date the origin of the Alphabet about 1800–1700 B.C.E., that is at about the beginning of the Hyksos period. The political situation of the Old World at that period favored the creation of a "revolutionary", "democratic" writing, in contradistinction to the "conservative", "theocratic" scripts of the old states of Mesopotamia and Egypt. The nationality of its inventors is unknown, but it is now generally agreed that they belonged to the North-West Semitic linguistic group.

Palestine and Syria, the geographical center of the greater Egypto-Mesopotamian civilization, offered conditions favorable to the invention and elaboration of alphabetic writing. Here was an area known to have been subject to many influences from the North-East (Mesopotamia) and the South-West (Egypt), from the North (Hittites), and the West (the Minoan civilization). Having received various elements of culture from the surrounding countries, the North-West Semites handed them on, somewhat elaborated and transformed, to other contiguous regions. Cuneiform, Egyptian and Minoan scripts, as well as prehistoric geometric symbols were known and used here, and were drawn upon for the new invention. Moreover, the language spoken in this region was particularly favorable to the creation of a consonantal alphabet.

WAS THE ALPHABET A HEBREW INVENTION?

It has been mentioned (p. 33 f.) that the Early Canaanite inscriptions—some going back to the period of the Patriarchs—may represent the original proto-type of the Alphabet. And, if there is substance in our theory that the twenty-two symbols of the original Alphabet were not pictographic but artificial and geometrical, and that the names were an artificial mnemotechnic device (p. 40), one is prompted to ask what seems a rather startling question: Did the Second Commandment (*Thou shalt not make unto thee any graven image, or any likeness of any thing* etc., etc.) play any part in the invention of the Alphabet? Or could it have been a pure coincidence that the North-Semitic alphabetic symbols were artificial and not representational, as nearly all the original non-alphabetic scripts were representational? In other words, is it possible that the ancient Hebrews who presented the World with the Bible and Monotheism, also gave it the Alphabet?

The possibility certainly exists, although it would not be easy to prove this thesis, apart from the generally accepted view that the Ten Commandments were probably promulgated about the 15th century B.C.E., whereas the Alphabet was probably invented about the 18th century B.C.E. On the other hand, it must be emphasized that Prof. N. H. Tur-Sinai has rightly attempted "to show ... that the basic concepts of the Israelitic faith are very much older than the Sinai legislation". However, it would be scientifically unwise to draw any definite conclusion.

The same may be said in connection with another theory advanced by Prof. Tur-Sinai in his articles *Who Created the Alphabet* (*The Palestine Post*, October 14 and 21, 1949) and *The Origin of the Alphabet* (*The Jewish Quarterly Review*, N.S. XLI, 1950–1, pp. 83–109, 159–79, and 277–301), as well as in his recent lecture (March, 1958) delivered to Jews' College, London. In Tur-Sinai's opinion, "The historic alphabet of twenty-two signs, as first developed and adapted to Hebrew and Aramaic, was created in Israel, for the purposes of Israel's religious law, and forms part of Israel's religious tradition". "Thus the alphabet as it was taught by priests in words and sentences from its very beginning, is a religious document, proclaiming the belief in one God." In other words, "the Canaanitic alphabet, beginning and foundation of all learning, is a creation of Israel's genius and a witness to the ancient origin of its *Torah*".

Tur-Sinai bases his attractive theory on certain Talmudic and early Christian explanations of the Hebrew letter-names. He argues that there was a Hebrew age-old tradition of teaching the alphabet-letters as "a didactic verse full of meaning and significance, a sublime literary, artistic and educational document". The substance of "that sublime didactic verse" was an injunction: "to love the Lord your God, to walk in all His ways and to cleave unto Him" or "Be like Him; even as He is compassionate and merciful, be you compassionate and merciful too."

Very attractive, very beautiful, but there is hardly any evidence to support the theory.

MAIN FEATURES OF THE ALPHABET

The great achievement in the creation of the Alphabet was not the invention of signs—ample evidence can be adduced for the invention of alphabets by schoolchildren who already know their ABC—but the inner working principle. This in its simplicity was the production of a system in which each sound was represented by one sign. The inventor of this system must, indeed, have been a very fine phonetician. For this achievement, simple as it now seems to us, the inventor is to be ranked among the greatest benefactors of mankind. No other people

38

in the world had been able to develop a true alphabetic system. "It was one, and only one, of the gifts of the Semites to mankind" (G. R. Driver). It was this alphabet which became the ancestor of all alphabetic scripts the world has known. Each civilization developed its own variation on the basic script and the passing of time has made the inter-relation of some members of the same family quite unrecognizable. Thus, the Brahmi script, the great mother-script of India, the Korean alphabet, the Mongolian scripts are derived from the same source as the Greek, the Latin, the Runic, the Hebrew, the Arabic, and the Russian alphabets, although it is practically impossible for a layman to see a real resemblance between them. See Pl. V–VI.

MAIN CHARACTERISTICS OF NORTH-SEMITIC ALPHABET

The N. Semitic alphabet remained almost unaltered for many centuries. Moreover, as mentioned in the Introduction, if we ignore the external form of the letters, and consider only their phonetic value, their number, and their order, we may regard the modern Hebrew alphabet as a continuation of the original North-Semitic alphabet, created more than 3,500 years ago.

The main characteristic of the N. Semitic alphabet is that it consisted of 22 letters or symbols, which correspond roughly to the first 22 letters of its offspring, the Greek alphabet. But the Semitic method of writing was, and still is, uniformly from right to left, and the 22 letters expressed consonants only, though some of them came to be used as long vowels. The absence of vowel-signs has not been satisfactorily explained. One theory is that the vowels were supplied locally, the sound given varying with the different dialects; in other words, the inventors left the vowels to be supplied according to local custom. It is pertinent to note how in English the same word is pronounced differently in different parts of the country, this being due rather to the varied methods of pronouncing vowels than to those of pronouncing consonants.

NAMES OF LETTERS

A few words about the names of the letters. The value of each consonant is the value of the first letter of its name (*b* of *beth*, *g* of *gimel*, *d* of *daleth*, etc.). This principle is known as *acrophony*. It would be wrong to assume that it necessarily indicates the use of pictorial representations of the objects whose names the letters bore: in other words, there is no clear evidence that the symbols were originally pictographic, that the letter *aleph* was an "ox's head on its side"; the *beth* a "house", the *gimel* a "camel", and so on. The names may have been applied to the signs, rather than being derived from the representation of the objects. The adoption of the names was, it seems, an artificial, mnemotechnic device, similar to those of modern *ABC*-books for children, in which—of course, independently of the form of the letter—*A* stands for "aeroplane" or "acorn" or "apple"; *B* for "bunny" or "bee" or "butterfly"; *C* for "cat" or "coat" or "candy".

ORDER OF LETTERS

The order of the modern Hebrew alphabet is the same as that of the original N. Semitic alphabet. That this is so can be proved by reference to acrostics in *Lament.* i–iv, *Prov.* xxxi. 10–31, *Psalms* xxv, xxxiv, cxi, cxii, and so on, to the Ugaritic *ABC*-tablet (see above), and to the early Greek, Etruscan, and Latin alphabets. In the excavations of the Wellcome-Marston Archaeological Expedition to the Near East at Lachish, in 1938, on the last day of the excavation a schoolboy's scribbling was found on the vertical face of the upper step of the staircase which led up to the Palace; it included the scratching of the first five letters of the Early Hebrew alphabet in their conventional order. The inscription probably belongs to the late ninth or early eighth century B.C.E. and is the first example of the Hebrew alphabet being learnt systematically.

The order of the letters of the N. Semitic alphabet gives an appearance of phonetic grouping, but this may be accidental. The meaning of the names seems to affect the arrangement.

In conclusion, although the overall picture seems to be clear, it must be stated that many aspects of the origin of the Alphabet are still in that twilight zone between conjecture and certainty, and many details of the general picture are still very far from settled.

CHAPTER 4

ALPHABET'S CONQUEST OF THE WORLD

Pl. V–VI

IN THE LATE second millennium and the early first millennium B.C.E., as in the early Hyksos period (see p. 36), the political situation in the ancient Near East was again confused. With the final or temporary political eclipse of the great nations of the Bronze Age, the Egyptians, the Assyrians, the Hittites, the Minoans, we enter a new historical world. In Palestine and Syria, three nations, Israel, Phoenicia and Aram, became increasingly important. To the south of the "Fertile Crescent", South-Arabian peoples attained a position of wealth and importance as the commercial intermediaries between the Mediterranean and the East. To the West, seeds were sown among the eager-minded peoples which later constituted the nation of Hellas, the Greeks.

These conditions favored the development of four branches of the Alphabet: South Semitic, Canaanite, Aramaic, and Greek.

SOUTH-SEMITIC BRANCH

The South-Semitic branch remained, generally speaking, confined within the Arabian Peninsula, where a number of pre-Islamic scripts developed. The numerous inscriptions extant are our main source, assisted by vague references in Classical writers, for the study of the once flourishing kingdoms whose splendor has been immortalized by the Biblical account of Solomon and the Queen of Sheba. By the time of the establishment of Islam, North Arabia had become more important than South Arabia. The later development of Islam wrecked the older civilization and relegated these fertile lands to the backwoods of history.

The Sabaean script spread into the African continent, where

it became the progenitor of the Ethiopic script, and so, of the modern Amharic, Tigré, Tigriña, and other scripts of Abyssinia, which are the only South-Semitic scripts still in use.

CANAANITE BRANCH
Pl. II

The Canaanite branch soon subdivided into (a) the Early Hebrew alphabet, which will be dealt with in Part II, and (b) the Phoenician and Punic alphabets, used by the Phoenicians in their mother-country and their colonies—Carthage, on the islands of Cyprus, Sardinia, Sicily, and so on. The scripts of the ancient Libyans and their descendants, the Berbers, and the Iberians were connected with the Punic alphabet.

ARAMAIC BRANCH

In the history of the Alphabet, the Aramaic branch occupies a place comparable with that of the Latin alphabet. With some exceptions, it is almost as if an agreement had been reached between those who used scripts belonging to or derived from the Canaanite and the Aramaic branches. All the alphabetic scripts west of Syria would seem to have derived, directly or indirectly, from the Canaanite, whereas the hundreds of alphabetic writings of the East apparently sprang from the Aramaic branch.

The Aramaic alphabet was probably developed in the tenth century B.C.E. for writing the language of the Aramaeans. This Semitic population had settled in a number of towns in Syria and Northern Mesopotamia, where they formed small independent states, which were conquered piecemeal by the Assyrians; the last one, Damascus, fell in 732 B.C.E. Although the Aramaeans were never politically important, from the seventh century B.C.E. onwards their language and their writing spread widely, and in the second half of the first millennium B.C.E. these became by far the most important and widespread language and script of the whole of Western Asia. Both language and script were officially adopted by the Persian Empire, and Aramaic monumental inscriptions and cursive documents have been unearthed in Egypt, Palestine, Syria, Arabia, Asia Minor, Mesopotamia and India.

OFFSHOOTS OF THE ARAMAIC BRANCH

In the late second century B.C.E. and during succeeding centuries numerous Aramaic offshoots became distinct entities. The direct and indirect descendants of the Aramaic alphabet can be divided into two main groups, those used for the Semitic and those for the non-Semitic languages.

ALPHABET FOLLOWS RELIGION

The first group comprises the following: (1) Hebrew (which will be dealt with in Part III); (2) Nabataean-Sinaitic-Arabic; (3) Palmyrene; (4) Syriac-Nestorian; (5) Mandaean; and (6) Manichaean. The aphorism *Alphabet follows Religion* applies more particularly to this group. It affects Hebrew as well as Arabic, but it also affects Syriac and Nestorian: the extremely active Nestorian missionaries carried their religious teaching, their Syriac language and their Syriac-Nestorian script into the Kurdistan highlands, into South India, into Turkestan, and amongst other Turki as well as Mongol tribes of Central Asia; from *c*. 630 onwards it even penetrated into China. The peculiar Mandaean script is the writing of a strange gnostic pagan-Jewish-Christian sect, known as Mandaeans or Nazaraeans, or Galileans or else Christians of St. John. The Manichaean was the script of the Manichaeans, whose religion from the middle of the third century A.D. onwards was for a millennium one of the most widely disseminated throughout the world. Finally, the Palmyrene script was the writing employed in ancient Palmyra, the Semitic Tadmor, an oasis-city on the trade route between Syria and Mesopotamia, which in the first three centuries of the Christian era became so powerful that she withstood mighty Rome.

ARABIC

The Arabic script apparently descended from the Aramaic through the Nabataean and the Neo-Sinaitic alphabets; after the Latin script it is nowadays the most generally used in Asia and Africa. Its diffusion is due to the fact that being the language and script of the Koran, the holy book of Islam, it spread with the expansion of this religion as far as West Africa and Central Africa, Southern Russia, India and Indonesia.

It has been adopted for and adapted to a great number of European and Asian languages and to various African tongues.

The evolution of the forms of the Arabic letters was the most rapid of all the branches of alphabetic writing. The Arabic alphabet probably originated in the fourth century C.E. and by the seventh century all its letters had completely changed their form. There are several styles of Arabic writing.

OTHER DESCENDANTS OF THE ARAMAIC ALPHABET

Numerous scripts of direct or indirect derivation from the Aramaic alphabet, have been adopted for, and adapted to non-Semitic languages of Central, Southern and South-Eastern Asia. These scripts may be distinguished into eight branches: (1) Kharoshthi, used from about the fourth century B.C.E. to about the fifth century C.E. in North-West India, Eastern Turkestan, and Eastern Afghanistan; (2) Persian or Iranian scripts, known as Pahlavi (including the Avesta alphabet), employed for the sacred, pre-Islamic Persian literature; (3) Sogdian, a language and script which in the second half of the first millennium C.E. were the *lingua franca* of Central Asia; (4) Kök Turki, a script used in the sixth–eighth centuries C.E. by early Turki tribes living in the southern part of Central Siberia, North-Western Mongolia, and North-Eastern Turkestan; a descendant of the Kök Turki was the Early Hungarian alphabet; (5) the script of the Uighurs, an important people of Turki speech, who lived in Mongolia and Eastern Turkestan; in the early thirteenth century the Uighur alphabet became the script of the Mongolian Empire; (6) the Mongolian branch, including Kalmuck, Buriat, Mongolian proper, and the allied Manchu alphabet; (7) the Armenian and Georgian alphabets: these were invented *c.* 400 C.E. by St. Mesrop; also the Caucasian Albanians (now extinct), had an allied alphabet; (8) Brahmi, the prototype of about 200 scripts now used in India, Tibet, Ceylon, Burma, Cambodia, Cochinchina, Siam, Indonesia, and to some little extent as far as the Philippine Islands; the Korean alphabet, which is the only native alphabet of the Far East, was indirectly derived from the Indian branch.

WESTERN BRANCH: THE GREEK ALPHABET AND ITS OFFSHOOTS

Pl. II and V-VI

Out of the troubled darkness which shrouded the transition from the Mycenaean civilization of the Late Bronze Age in the twelfth century B.C.E. to the Early Greek primitive geometric art of the Iron Age, tenth-ninth century B.C.E.—there came the remarkable invention of the Greek alphabet, the earliest fully-developed alphabetic system of writing, containing both consonants and vowels. The North-Semitic origin of the Greek alphabet is accepted by all serious scholars. The origin is proved by these facts: (1) the shapes of nearly all the Early Greek letters and of the derivative Etruscan letters clearly recall their Semitic origin; (2) the phonetic value of the majority of the Early Greek letters was the same as that of the Semitic letters; (3) the order of the Greek letters corresponds, with a few understandable exceptions, to the order of the Semitic letters; (4) the direction of writing in the Early Greek script, and in the derivative Etruscan script, was from right to left as in the Semitic; and (5) the names of the letters: whereas the Greek names are meaningless in Greek, the Semitic names of the letters are generally words in the Semitic languages.

Much more difficult is the chronological problem. There are many conflicting opinions concerning the date of borrowing of the Greek alphabet: they range between the fourteenth and the seventh centuries B.C.E. There is no direct evidence for any of the dates suggested, but inferences point to about 1000 B.C.E. if not earlier as the time of the introduction of the alphabet into Greece.

DEVELOPMENT OF THE GREEK ALPHABET

The Greeks made several important changes in the alphabet, the greatest being the transformation of the purely consonantal Semitic script into a modern alphabet containing vowels. They twice changed the direction of writing: for a certain period they employed the *boustrophedon* style (a Greek term meaning alternately from right to left and from left to right, as the ox draws the plough), but after 500 B.C.E. they wrote invariably from left to right and from top to bottom. They gave the script symmetry and art. In time, from the classical monumental

45

alphabet, always used for inscriptions, there sprang the Greek uncial script, the cursive hands, and the minuscule, which was adapted as a book-hand about 800 C.E. Out of the cursive hands, there gradually developed the modern Greek minuscule. The capitals of modern Greek handwriting are partly borrowed from the Latin.

OFFSHOOTS OF THE GREEK BRANCH

Through its direct and indirect descendants, the Etruscan and Latin alphabets on the one hand and the Cyrillic alphabet of the Slavs on the other, the Greek has become the progenitor of all the European alphabets. In the course of its long history it had other offshoots too, among them various alphabets of ancient Asia Minor including the Lycian, the Phrygian, the Pamphylian, the Lydian, and the Carian alphabets; and one important African alphabet, that of the Copts--the indigenous population of Egypt, who after the Arabic conquest of that country in 641, continued to maintain their Christian monophysite religion; the Coptic language and script are still used for liturgical purposes. Another important offshoot was the Gothic alphabet, invented by Bishop Ulfilas (fourth century C.E.), mainly on the basis of the Greek uncial script, with some influence, however, of the Roman character and of the Runes, which will be discussed further on.

SLAVONIC ALPHABETS: ALPHABET
FOLLOWS RELIGION

Two alphabets, the Cyrillic and the Glagolitic, were employed for writing the early Slavonic language. They differed widely in the form and to some extent in the number of their letters, and in the history of their development, but they were alike in representing adequately the many sounds of the Slavonic language and were richer than any other European alphabet. The Cyrillic alphabet, based on the Greek uncial alphabet of the ninth century, developed in course of time into the national scripts of those Slavonic peoples who accepted their religion from Byzantium, namely the Russians, White Russians, Ukrainians, Bulgarians, Serbs. Further, through the Russian script this alphabet has been adopted for several Finno-Ugrian, Turki and Iranian languages. While the invention of the Cyrillic script is generally attributed to St.

Cyril, we cannot exclude the possibility that this theory is based on a late tradition, because the early tradition, in attributing to St. Cyril the invention of an early Slavonic writing, does not indicate whether this was the Cyrillic or the Glagolitic. The latter or both may have been invented by St. Cyril.

ORIGIN OF THE LATIN ALPHABET
Pl. II

It is a somewhat curious fact that few examples of the Latin alphabet (also known as the Roman character), which is so important in the history of civilization, survive from the first five or six centuries of its existence. The oldest record of its use extant, on a gold brooch known as the Praeneste fibula, belongs to the seventh century B.C.E. There are two sixth-century inscriptions, and a few of the following centuries. Only from the first century B.C.E. onwards are Latin inscriptions too numerous and too widespread geographically to be counted.

The general opinion used to be, and many still hold, that the Latin alphabet derived directly from the Greek in the form used by the Greek colonists in Italy. Recently, however, it has been shown that this theory is improbable and that the link between the Greek and the Latin was in fact the Etruscan alphabet. Most of the Latin letter names (such as *a, be, ce, de,* for the Greek *alpha, beta, gamma, delta*), which have descended into English as into the majority of modern alphabets, were also taken over from the Etruscans.

ETRUSCAN ALPHABET
Pl. II

The Etruscans, a highly civilized people and the ancestors of the modern Tuscans, were the predecessors of the Romans; their language, still undeciphered, has come down to us in about nine thousand inscriptions, the earliest being the eighth-century B.C.E. Marsiliana Tablet, which is the earliest preserved Western *ABC*. Like the Semitic and the early Greek alphabets, the Etruscan writing nearly always reads from right to left. The early Etruscan alphabet, unlike any early Greek alphabet preserved in the Greek inscriptions which have come down to

47

us, contains the original, the prototype Greek alphabet, consisting of the 22 North-Semitic letters with the phonetic values given to them by the Greeks, and the four additional purely Greek letters at the end of the alphabet. We may thus assume that the Etruscan alphabet originated from a remote primitive Greek alphabet employed before subdivision into the Eastern and Western groups, which are well known from the inscriptions extant. The Etruscans introduced various changes in their script, and several features in the present alphabet are due to the influence of the ancient Etruscans: it will suffice to refer to the *k*-phonetic value of *c*, *k* and *q* in the modern English alphabet.

The Etruscan alphabet had several varieties and many off-shoots. Amongst the former, we may mention the North-Etruscan or Alpine alphabets employed in the Alpine valleys. Amongst the off-shoots, there were, apart from the Latin, several alphabets used by the Italic populations of pre-Roman Italy and also by non-Italic tribes. The Runes, the "national" scripts of some Gothic and North Germanic tribes, which were also used by the Anglo-Saxons in the British Isles, may have originated about the first century B.C.E. from a North Etruscan alphabet. The Oghamic alphabet, peculiar to the Celtic population of the British Isles, may have originated in the fourth century C.E. in South Wales or South Ireland, but its source is uncertain.

DEVELOPMENT OF THE LATIN ALPHABET
Pl. II

Of the Greek-Etruscan letters the Romans adopted only 21; the other three became numbers (*theta* became $C = 100$; *phi* became $M = 1000$, and its half became $D = 500$; *khi* became $L = 50$). Later a few other changes were introduced: the ancient *zeta* was dropped and was replaced by a G (by adding a bar to C), and in the first century B.C.E. the symbols Y and Z were adopted for the transliteration of Greek sounds, and were placed at the end of the alphabet. The subsequent history of the Latin alphabet consisted essentially in the external transformation of the single letters, especially in the cursive or current styles of writing. The monumental alphabet remained practically unaltered and in late medieval times was taken over for the majuscules. In the Middle Ages, too, there was some further change: the signs *U–V* were differentiated and *W* was added; also *I–J* were differentiated.

LATIN: ALPHABET FOLLOWS RELIGION

The Latin language and script were carried by Roman legionaries and imperial officials to all parts of the vast Roman Empire, particularly to the regions which were not Hellenized. In a few countries, Latin replaced the language of the natives, and it thus became the ancestor of the modern Romance languages, particularly Italian, French, Spanish, Portuguese and Roumanian, all of which sooner or later adopted the Latin alphabet. At a later stage and during many more centuries, churchmen and missionaries carried the Latin language and script still further afield. Catholic Rome was then the light of the Western world, the center whence religion and learning were disseminated to all parts of Western, Central and Northern Europe. In consequence, Latin, with its Latin alphabet, the language of the Roman Church, became and remained for many centuries the *lingua franca* of the European higher intellectual world, and is still used extensively for learned works and theological treatises in the Roman Catholic Church, and also, though to a lesser degree, in medicine and jurisprudence. The ascendancy of Latin led to the adoption of the Latin alphabet by a large majority of nations, and it was adapted to tongues of the most diverse linguistic groups.

"NATIONAL" LITERARY HANDS

When the various European countries had shaken off the political authority of Rome, and the learned communities had been dissolved, and its members scattered, a marked change took place in the development of the Latin literary or book-hand. Several "national" hands, or rather styles of the Latin cursive minuscule, assumed distinctive features. There thus developed on the European continent and in the British Isles the five basic "national" hands, each giving rise to several varieties—Italian, Merovingian (in France), Visigothic (in Spain), Germanic, and "Insular" or Anglo-Irish hands. At the end of the eighth century the Caroline or Carolingian hand developed and, having become the official script and literary hand of the Frankish Empire, during the next two centuries became the main literary writing style of Western Europe. The combination of majuscules (or capital letters) and minuscules (or small letters) is due mainly to the Caroline script.

BLACK-LETTER, ROMAN TYPE AND ITALICS
Pl. II

In the course of the next centuries various book-hands, court-hands or chart-hands and other cursive scripts developed from the Caroline. The changes were not always for the better. Before the invention of printing, a wholly new fashion in letters was to spread across much of Europe. This was the style known as black-letter or "Gothic", developed from the Caroline hand; it was almost universally used, but it took different forms in different countries. Italy preferred a rounder form, called by the Italians, not quite properly, *littera antiqua*, which we know as "humanistic" script.

In about 1450 there came the invention of printing at a time when two main sorts of letters were being used in Europe: the black-letter in Germany and the *littera antiqua* in Italy. Gutenberg himself, probably the earliest European printer with movable types, copied the black letter; so did Caxton, the first English printer. But Gutenberg's invention was soon taken to Italy, and there the *littera antiqua* was used by Sweynheym and Pannartz, who had come from Germany, and by the Frenchman Nicolas Jenson, the great Venetian printer, who perfected what we now call the "Roman" type. There was also a cursive form of the humanistic hand, with sloping letters and some joins between them. This style, which became the source of our modern *italics*, was perfected in Venice by Aldus Manutius, who founded a great family business which lasted for a hundred years. The use of the "Roman" type and of *italics* spread all over the world. They were brought into England from Italy in the sixteenth century. Today, Germany is the only country in which there is a living tradition for the use of black-letter, but even there in the last half-a-century there has been a slow change towards the use of the "Roman" and *italic* design.

50

MODERN WESTERN ALPHABETS

The "national" modern alphabets of the Western nations are, strictly speaking, adaptations of the Latin alphabet to Germanic (English, German, Swedish, Danish, etc.), Romance (Italian, French, Spanish, etc.), Slavonic (Polish, Czech, etc.), Finno-Ugrian languages (Finnish, Hungarian, etc.), Baltic (Lithuanian, Lettish), and other languages. But the adaptation of a script to a language is not easy, especially when the language contains sounds which do not occur in the speech from which the script has been borrowed. There arises, therefore, the difficulty of representing the new sounds. This difficulty was met quite differently in various alphabets. For instance, the sound *shch* (as in "Ashchurch"), which in Russian is represented by one sign (ш), is represented in Czech by two signs (*šč*), in Polish by four (*szcz*), in English likewise by four, though different, signs (*shch*), and in German by as many as seven (*schtsch*).

ENGLISH SPELLING

This brings us to the problem of phonetic spelling and the much-discussed necessity of spelling reform. Very few alphabets are what we may call "perfect"; such an alphabet would imply the accurate rendering of all speech-sounds: each sound would be represented by a single, constant symbol, and not more than one sound by the same symbol. In English, for instance, the number of the ancient Roman letters was from the beginning insufficient to express with accuracy all the sounds (there are no single letters to represent the sounds *th*, *sh*, *ch*), while several letters are redundant (*q* and *c* when representing the sound *k*). As a result, while English is probably the richest and the most colorful of all modern languages, English spelling differs so much from pronunciation that in many words it is almost an arbitrary symbolism. What better example of the English spelling-problem can be given than the following sentence containing ten different pronunciations of *ough* ("uff", "oe", "ow", "off", "up", "oo", "ock", "â", "aw", "o"): "The *rough*-headed *dough*-faced pl*ough*man went c*ough*ing and hic*ough*ing thr*ough* the village after h*ough*ing the thor*ough*bred which he had b*ough*t for his br*ough*am."

PART II

EARLY HEBREW ALPHABET
Pl. II–X

CHAPTER 1

EARLY HEBREW INSCRIPTIONS AND DEVELOPMENT OF THE EARLY HEBREW ALPHABET

Pl. II–IV and VII–X

BIBLICAL CRITICS OF the last century did not believe that any system of writing was employed by the Hebrews, or indeed by the Semites of Palestine and surrounding districts, as early as the age of Moses. On the other hand, some fanciful Jewish Bible exegete tried to interpret the verse *az huḥàl liqrò beshèm YHWH* (*Gen.* iv. 26), as if writing were invented in the time of Enosh, the son of Seth. Of certain importance, however, is the Biblical passage of *Exod.* xvii. 14 (cf. also xxxiv. 27): ". . . Write this for a memorial in a book and rehearse it in the ears of Joshua. . . ."

THEORIES OF BIBLICAL CRITICS

Winckler, Naville, Benzinger, Jeremias, Grimme, and other eminent scholars of the last hundred years argued that the cuneiform was the official mode of writing of ancient Israel up to the time of Hezekiah (*c.* 700 B.C.E.). Some parts of the Bible were supposed to have been written in cuneiform characters on clay tablets, and certain Biblical terms have been interpreted accordingly. Other scholars, too, denied that alphabetic writing was practiced in Palestine before the Persian period. Dr. Cowley suggested that it was Ezra who, with the assistance of his colleagues, translated the cuneiform documents into Hebrew, and wrote the result down in the simple Aramaic characters.

Jewish scholars, on the other hand, suggested that the Square Hebrew alphabet, the ancestor of modern Hebrew writing, was employed unchanged from the time of Moses. The great Jewish-Italian savant Azaria de' Rossi was the first to assert, on the basis of several statements in the Talmudic literature

55

bearing on the Torah text, that the Torah was originally written in the Early Hebrew script, *ketabh 'ibhrî*.

It has to be emphasized that until relatively recent times, the epigraphical remains of ancient Israel were very scarce. Until this very day no Israelite *stelae* (monumental stones) of victory like those of the Egyptians or Babylonians or Assyrians, or even of the Moabites or Aramaeans, have been unearthed. David, Solomon, Jeroboam, Hezekiah, Isaiah, Jeremiah, and all the other kings of Israel or Judah and the other great prophets are known to us primarily from the Biblical record.

SCARCITY OF HEBREW INSCRIPTIONS

This paucity of ancient Israelite written documents has been accounted for in various ways. Some historians belittle the enterprise of ancient Israel and the culture of poor, little Palestine; the Hebrews are said to have possessed none of the political, administrative, and civic genius for "imperial conquest". Another opinion suggests that the numerous invasions of Palestine must have been responsible for the destruction of her inscriptions; or that the pre-exilic inscriptions were not allowed to survive, because they appeared unorthodox to later Judaism.

In the light of present evidence, however, the following two theories are the most probable: (1) until a quarter of a century ago, excavations in Palestine were not conducted in accordance with rigid scientific method, and many small inscriptions, of the size of several Lachish ostraca or, more particularly, seals, may have been lost for ever. (2) The vast majority of the contemporary documents, and particularly all literary works, were written upon papyrus, imported from Egypt, or on parchment; in the soil of Palestine, which, save for the dry district of the Dead Sea, is generally damp, no papyrus or parchment could be expected to have endured until our time, unless preserved in conditions similar to those of the recently discovered Dead Sea scrolls; *Jer.* xxxii. 14 refers to a similar practice in earlier times. The discovery at Lachish of several clay impressions which have on the back traces of the papyrus documents to which they had been attached, testifies to the use of this writing material for commercial and other purposes: see also p. 79 f.

There can be no doubt that there were many Early Hebrew

56

documents, but the vast majority have been destroyed, some perhaps by human agency, a great deal more probably by the action of time and climate, and others possibly in other ways. There is, of course, the possibility that future excavations will unearth many more inscriptions and also documents written on perishable materials preserved in some dry locality.

EARLY HEBREW INSCRIPTIONS

In spite of the scantiness of material and the absence of long inscriptions, the history of the Early Hebrew writing is being gradually unfolded in a marvellous way. The term "Early Hebrew" is employed for the writing of ancient Israel in pre-exilic times—though some scholars prefer the term "Old Hebrew" and others "Hebrew-Phoenician"—and is used in contradistinction to the term "Square Hebrew", which will be discussed in Part III. In Talmudic literature, and in the early Christian writings based on this literature, Early Hebrew writing is generally referred to as *ketabh 'ibhrî*, "Hebrew script", although the terms *libbona'ah* and *r'ṣ* or *d'ṣ*, of uncertain origin and meaning, are also occasionally found.

During the past fifty years there has been a considerable amount of research on Early Hebrew inscriptions. In his outstanding *Text-book of North-Semitic Inscriptions* (Oxford University Press, 1903), Prof. G. A. Cooke included only one Early Hebrew inscription and three Early Hebrew seals. Thirty years later, about three hundred Early Hebrew inscriptions, including ostraca, inscribed seals and weights, were published by the present writer in *Le iscrizioni antico-ebraiche palestinesi* (Florence University, 1934). In the last twenty years many more Early Hebrew ostraca, seals, jar-handle stamps, weights, inscribed parchment-fragments or papyri, and various other fragments have been discovered and Early Hebrew epigraphy brought within the reach of the ordinary reader.

With the increase in the number of these documents, our knowledge of Early Hebrew epigraphy steadily increases. We are now able to trace in the Early Hebrew alphabet the gradual change which throws light on the independent development of all known alphabets. Within limits, we can now be reasonably certain about the nationality and the date of important inscriptions.

57

IMPORTANCE OF EARLY HEBREW
INSCRIPTIONS

The nature of the Early Hebrew documents—although the great majority consist of only one or two words—is noteworthy. What is recorded is for the most part not the history of great events or of striking personalities, but the details of everyday life. Even the smallest documents furnish information which is of considerable value in supplementing our knowledge of the Bible, and of the life and customs of ancient Israel.

For instance, the ostraca of Samaria, which contain various data regarding the nature and provenance of supplies of wine and refined oil, and are probably dockets relating to payments of taxes in kind to the palace of Samaria, throw much light on the language, religion, and personal names of the inhabitants of the Northern Kingdom in the eighth century B.C.E. as well as on its topography, and especially on its provincial and fiscal administration, of which very little was previously known. Philologically, these documents are extremely important as they represent the earliest preserved texts written in the Hebrew dialect of the Northern Kingdom. In them we have the form *yn* (or *yen*) instead of the Biblical *y y n* (*yayyin*), "wine", and *sh t* instead of the Biblical *sh n t* or *sh n h* (*shenath* or *shanah*), "year".

While the Samarian ostraca provide us with examples of the script and dialect of the Kingdom of Israel, most of the other inscriptions illustrate those of Judah. These include the inscription of Siloam, attributed to *c.* 700 B.C.E., and the Lachish Letters, written during Jeremiah's lifetime in about the beginning of 587 B.C.E. Some of the Judaean documents contain new words or interesting forms, but on the whole the style in these inscriptions is pure and idiomatic, and reads like a good prose passage from the Hebrew Bible.

JAR-HANDLE STAMPS AND SEALS

The jar-handle seal-impressions known as the "Royal jar-handle stamps"—because they contain the word *l m l k* or *la-melekh* ("to the King", "of the King", "belonging to the King", or "Royal"), in addition to one of the four city-names Hebron, Ziph, Sokoh, and the unidentified *MMSHT*—are interesting as they show that the jars in question were made in the royal factories (which are probably those mentioned in 1 *Chr.* iv. 23). They will be discussed on p. 70 ff.

Various seals contain the designation *'ebed ha-melekh*, "Servant of the King", a term which occurs frequently in the Bible; there is sufficient evidence to show that the phrase does not mean "servant" or "slave", but "minister" or other high official. A similar term found on seals is *ben ha-melekh* ("Son of the King"), as well as *na'ar*, literally "Boy", both meaning "minister" or "high official".

Another seal is inscribed with the title *'asher 'al ha-bayith*, —"He Who is Over the Household", "the Majordomo", "the Chief Steward"—which is also a well-known Biblical term. One seal contains the representation of a fighting cock, which is the earliest Palestinian representation of this fowl, and fills a gap in our knowledge of the life of ancient Israel: cocks are not mentioned in the Bible, and it was hitherto stated that in Palestine they were not known in Biblical times.

These and other seals will be discussed on p. 73 f.

INSCRIBED WEIGHTS

Of the Early Hebrew inscribed weights, nearly thirty have come down to us. These are of great interest for the student of the Bible, both from the metrological and the philological standpoints; but again their contribution to our knowledge of the development of Early Hebrew writing is not very great, though several specimens contain letters in rather unusual forms.

The two weights most often mentioned in the Bible are the *kikkar*, or "talent", and *shekel*, but no Early Hebrew weight which has been found bears the inscription *kikkar*, and only one, and a rather doubtful one at that, is inscribed *shekel*. There are, however, seven bearing the inscription *beqa'* (cf. *Gen.* xxiv. 22 and *Exod.* xxxviii. 26).

Fourteen Early Hebrew weights bear the inscription *neṣeph*, a hitherto unknown metrological term, and seven are inscribed with the term *pîm*, a puzzling word which appears in 1 *Sam.* xiii. 21. Until the discovery of the *pîm*-weights, this passage had puzzled all translators of the Bible, but now the obscurity is cleared up; we know that in this passage *pîm* indicates a weight and expresses the price which the Israelites had to pay to the Philistines for the sharpening of their ploughshares, axes, etc.

The Early Hebrew inscribed weights also show that "divers" weights were employed, "just and unjust", as the Biblical passages indicate (*Lev.* xix. 35 f.; *Deut.* xxv. 13 ff., etc.). They also show that the Early Hebrew metrological system was far more complicated than had hitherto been supposed, and we may assume that there were independent systems, which varied locally and probably also according to the goods for sale, just as nowadays in England the chemist, the grocer, and the jeweller use different standards.

EARLY HEBREW ALPHABET
Pl. III

Like current Hebrew, the Early Hebrew alphabet contained 22 letters. Their names probably corresponded with the current names: *'aleph, beth, gimel, daleth, he, waw, zayin, ḥeth, ṭeth, yod, kaph, lamed, mem, nun, samekh, 'ayin, pe, ṣade, qoph, resh, shin, taw.* The value of each letter was that of the first letter of its name (*b, g, d*, etc.), but the exact phonetic value of letters such as *'ayin, ṣade*, and *shin* has been lost.

The Early Hebrew alphabet was strictly related to the other North-Semitic alphabets, particularly to the early Phoenician and the early Aramaic. The Moabite, the Edomite, and the Ammonite alphabets may be regarded as secondary branches of the Early Hebrew, while the Samaritan alphabet and the Jewish coin-script of the Maccabaean period and of the period of the Bar Kochba war were its direct offshoots.

The main characteristics of the Early Hebrew letters are by now clearly established. Comparing, for instance, the Early Hebrew letters with the Phoenician, we see that the former, and particularly the *zayin* and *ṣade*, are more squat, wider and shorter, also more accurate.

The main strokes of the Early Hebrew *kaph, lamed, mem, nun, pe*, and sometimes also *beth*, are curved or rounded at the bottom. In the *ḥeth* the vertical strokes go beyond the horizontal ones. In the *he* the upper horizontal stroke goes beyond the vertical, and in some inscriptions the *he* has four horizontal strokes instead of three (strangely enough, a similar feature appears in the Etruscan alphabet). *Zayin* and *ṣade* curve back at the end of the lower horizontal stroke.

There are often some beautiful ligatures; these are generally of two letters, though there is an interesting instance of a

60

ligature of three letters. It may be assumed that these characteristics are due mainly to the influence of the cursive writing, though they also appear in Early Hebrew inscriptions.

DIFFICULTIES IN DEFINING THE DEVELOPMENT OF EARLY HEBREW WRITING

The historian of Early Hebrew writing is at a very great disadavantage as compared with the Greek or Latin epigraphist or palaeographer. Tens of thousands of Greek and Latin inscriptions are extant; in addition, a great number of specimens of Greek and Latin hand-writing have come down to us. Thanks to the vast amount of material, we are able to divide the study of Greek and Latin writing into two departments: (1) Epigraphy, the science concerned with the study of inscriptions, and (2) Palaeography, the science which seeks to read and to interpret writings in ink on perishable materials, such as papyrus, parchment, or paper, and, occasionally, on sherds or wax. Nevertheless, we are in the same difficulty with regard to the early history of the Greek and Latin alphabets as we are with the Hebrew. Moreover, it must be remembered that in the last pre-Christian centuries when Greek and particularly Latin inscriptions and written documents became very numerous (see p. 47), Early Hebrew writing had already passed out of common use.

At any rate, in the case of Early Hebrew, owing to the dearth of material, we are not in a position to subdivide this study into Epigraphy and Palaeography. But as the greater part of the Early Hebrew documents are inscriptions, their study in practice belongs to the field of Epigraphy. With the increase in the number of documents found to be extant, however, our knowledge of Early Hebrew Epigraphy also steadily increases. To delineate the development of the Early Hebrew writing, we must of course start with a discussion of its origin.

ORIGIN OF EARLY HEBREW ALPHABET
Pl. II– III

The Early Hebrew alphabet probably goes back to the birth of the Hebrew nation. In its earliest stage, the Early Hebrew

61

alphabet is identical with the North-Semitic alphabet before the latter's subdivision into the main branches set out on p. 41. Hence, the problem of the origin of the Early Hebrew alphabet practically corresponds with the problem of the origin of the North-Semitic alphabet (see p. 35 ff). There is thus a possibility that the Early Canaanite script (see p. 33 f.) may have been the prototype of the Early Hebrew alphabet. In that case, the Alphabet may already have been in use in the days of the Patriarchs.

Might this not be a further reason for thinking that the signet-ring of Judah (*Gen.* xxxviii. 18 and 25) was inscribed in the Early Canaanite writing, or else in another prototype of the Early Hebrew alphabet? It is true that this signet-ring may not have been inscribed at all, but in view of what we read in *Exod.* xxviii. 21 and 36, we may assume that inscribed signet-rings existed in very early times.

I do not think that there can be any doubt that alphabetic writing was used in the time of Moses, but unless it was a script allied to that of the Early Canaanite inscriptions referred to on p. 33 f., we cannot know what characters were employed. Several Biblical passages refer incidentally to writing in that period (*Exod.* xvii. 14; xxviii. 21 and 36, etc.), and it is highly probable that it was alphabetic; for the period of the Judges there is another casual Biblical reference to writing. It is worth emphasizing that such incidental references are as a rule more trustworthy than formal or elaborate expositions. In *Judges* viii. 14 we read of Gideon that "He caught a young man of the men of Succoth, and enquired of him; and he wrote down for him the princes of Succoth, and the elders thereof, seventy and seven men". We may assume from this passage that already in Gideon's time (twelfth or eleventh century, B.C.E.) an acquaintance with the art of writing (and most probably of alphabetic writing) had spread even amongst sections of the country population. This opinion receives support from the Gezer Calendar and from the Lachish *incunabula*, to be dealt with further on.

No doubt, there was some illiteracy; even of a much later period (the time of Isaiah, eighth century B.C.E.) we are told: "And the writing is delivered to him that is not learned, saying 'Read this, I pray thee', and he saith 'I am not learned' " (*Isaiah* xxix. 12). It is probable that at an early date there were professional scribes, and even organized guilds of scribes,

62

though the passage *Judg.* v. 14 on which this theory is based is rather obscure. Furthermore, the passage 1 *Chr.* ii. 55: "And the families of scribes that dwelt at Jabeṣ, the Tirathites, the Shime'athites, the Sucathites . . ." would seem to suggest that the profession of scribe was hereditary.

A recently deciphered fragmentary inscription, found in 1938 at Lachish and dated to the late twelfth or early eleventh century B.C.E., may, if the present writer's decipherment is correct, be regarded as the *incunabula* of the Early Hebrew writing. Only part of the inscription is preserved; the three or four signs may be read *la'ûth*.

More famous is the Gezer Calendar of eight lines, already referred to, which is generally assigned to the period of Saul or David (*c.* 1000 B.C.E.). It is a small soft-stone tablet, discovered in 1908 at Gezer, in S. Israel, on which is inscribed a sort of agricultural calendar beginning in October, or rather a list of eight months with the agricultural operation for each. According to some scholars it was the work of a peasant; according to others it is a schoolboy's exercise tablet. Be that as it may, we can assume that *c.* 1000 B.C.E. after the united kingdom had been established, and its centralized administration organized by King David, assisted by a staff of secretaries (see 2 *Sam.* viii. 17; xx. 25; and elsewhere), the Early Hebrew alphabet was already in existence and had begun its autonomous development. See Pl. IV-VI.

DEVELOPMENT OF EARLY HEBREW ALPHABET
Pl. III

The development of the single letters was, like that of the Phoenician and Early Aramaic alphabets, but unlike the Greek or Latin and many other alphabets, including the English, purely external, that is in the shape of the letters. Indeed, throughout the period of the employment of the Early Hebrew alphabet, for about a thousand years, the number and phonetic value of its letters remained the same.

Even the external development of the Early Hebrew letters is not as evident as in other scripts. On the whole, the Early Hebrew alphabet was so constant, that hardly any of its letters changed form so radically that even a layman could mistake their identity.

63

In the opinion of the present writer, this is a most significant phenomenon; indeed, it is probably unique in the history of ancient writing. One may speculate as to its causes—there is, of course, the obvious reason that this alphabet was so well adapted to the Hebrew language that there was no particular need to introduce changes. For instance, there may have been a central education system, providing for a fairly close inter-communication between various parts of the country and the various classes of society; or a fairly widespread study of at least the earliest Biblical books or literature in general, in which case their original script would doubtless have served as a model for all forms of writing.

We know from the Bible that even children learned to write: "And the remnant of the trees of his forest shall be few, that a child may write them down" (*Isaiah* x. 19). We also know that King Jehoshaphat "in the third year of his reign sent to his princes . . . to teach in the cities of Judah" (2 *Chr*. xvii. 7).

In Lachish, in 1938, on the last day of the excavations, an inscription was discovered on the steps of the Palace. The signs, together with a rough drawing of a lion, were so faintly scratched in the soft limestone, that the excavators could only see them in a side light. The main importance of this inscription lies in the fact that it included the first five letters of the Early Hebrew alphabet in their conventional order ('*aleph*, *beth*, *gimel*, *daleth*, *he*).

The excavators recognized straight away that it might be the work of a schoolboy airing his knowledge, writing the equivalent of ABCDE. This is actually the earliest archaeo-logical evidence for the order of the alphabet in Palestine, and the first example of the Hebrew alphabet being learnt systematically. On palaeographic grounds—the *daleth* has a short tail, the tall form of the *beth*, the *he* in which the upper horizontal stroke does not pass the vertical line of the letter—this inscription may be assigned to the late ninth or the early eighth century B.C.E., that is not long after the reign of Jehoshaphat (see above).

Separation of words by spaces is not found in Early Hebrew documents any more than it is in any other alphabetic inscrip-tion before the Roman period. With few exceptions, the words are separated by dots or little strokes. In the Gezer Calendar, however, there are no word-dividers, but longer strokes separate the clauses when these do not terminate at the end of the line. In the *Leviticus* fragments (see further on) two empty spaces serve as verse- or section-dividers, as in the Massoretic text of the Bible which we use today. Words at the end of a line are split between that line and the next, the word-division never being marked.

STYLES OF EARLY HEBREW WRITING
Pl. III

As we have said, despite the advance in the study of Early Hebrew inscriptions, it is still not easy to delineate the exact history of the development of the Early Hebrew alphabet. This is due not only to the dearth of preserved material, but also to the relative constancy of the shapes of the letters. Therefore, instead of attempting to describe the chronological development of the Early Hebrew alphabet, it will be more interesting and practical to attempt a classification, according to the style of writing, of the material which has come down to us.

Early Hebrew written documents, like those of any civilized nation, ancient or modern, may be subdivided into two main classes: (1) inscriptions written in monumental style, and (2) documents written in letters of cursive form.

Moreover, it is common knowledge that before the invention of printing any developed handwriting had broadly two styles, the ordinary cursive or current hand, common to all, employed for everyday life, and the carefully written literary or book-hand employed by trained scribes for copying literary works. Not that the two classes were always kept distinct; books were copied in current hand by a scholar for private study, and quite often the original was written in that hand by the author himself. On the other hand, documents which would more often be written in the current hand, may for some official reason have been written in a set form of writing or book-hand, and this hand may also have been employed sometimes for more important official letters or even for private correspondence. These are, however, exceptional cases. Generally speaking, there always existed a certain conflict between the book-hand and the natural current hand.

We now know that in ancient Israel, too, there were two cursive styles, the current hand and the literary or book-hand.

Thus, on the whole we can distinguish the following styles of writing in the Early Hebrew alphabet: (1) monumental or lapidary; (2) current hand; and (3) literary or book-hand.

It need hardly be said that the three styles were based on the same alphabet and were used concurrently. The original Early Hebrew alphabet was probably composed of letters of a defined though rough character, but different writing materials and tools favored different kinds of characters, and the different purposes of the intended document set before the scribe or calligrapher different artistic ideals or utilitarian needs; the same thing applied in some measure to the stone scribe-cutter.

CHAPTER 2

MONUMENTAL SCRIPTS

Pl. III–IV and VII

THE CHIEF CONSIDERATION of Early Hebrew monumental writing, as in any other lapidary style of writing, was permanence and beauty, including proportion and evenness. The characters when inscribed or incised on stone, as a rule stood as separate units, without ligatures, and if set down with care and uniformity would become the letters now considered to be in monumental style. On the whole, the letters tended to be made up of independent strokes or scratches of the chisel, with as few curves as possible. These general features of monumental scripts, however, do not entirely apply to examples of Early Hebrew, at least not to the main inscription—indeed, the only one which can be considered an inscription in the full sense—the Siloam inscription (see also p. 69 f.).

GEZER CALENDAR

Pl. III–IV and V–VI

This interesting document, already referred to several times, may be regarded as the starting point of the history of the Early Hebrew script. The majority of its letters are probably identical or nearly identical with those of the original Early Hebrew alphabet. The letters, throughout, have archaic forms. The letter *mem* still retains the probably original zig-zag form; the *samekh* is of the earliest type, its main feature being that the perpendicular stroke starts from above the top horizontal stroke, a peculiarity representing an earlier type than the *samekh* of the Moabite Stone (see below). The forms of the letters *aleph*, *daleth*, *waw*, *qoph*, and *shin* are also archaic.

The main features of the Early Hebrew letters, such as the curving of the shafts of the letters, the secondary and the supplementary additions, the overlapping, intersection, and prolongation of the strokes, are either lacking altogether or appear in a very slight degree. The forms of the letters *mem*, *pe*, *ṣade*, and *qoph* are quite different from those, for instance,

67

of the Siloam inscription (see below). However, several signs of the Gezer Calendar have assumed forms which foreshadow the subsequent characteristic shapes of the Early Hebrew letters. Thus, for example, the letters *kaph, mem, nun* and *pe* exhibit a tendency to bend their main stems to the left.

MESHA' STELE (See Pl. II)

The next stage in the development of the Early Hebrew monumental style may be reconstructed from an inscription in an allied script, the Moabite Stone, also known as the Mesha' Stele. This famous victory-stele, discovered in 1868 at Dibon, some 25 miles East of the Dead Sea, and now, partly restored, in the Museum of the Louvre, is a self-glorification of Mesha', king of Moab (2 *Kings* iii. 4) and belongs to about the middle of the ninth century B.C.E. Until the discovery of the Ahiram epitaph (see p. 35 f.) it was regarded as the earliest inscription in alphabetic writing. The inscription is of considerable importance; from the historical standpoint it supplements the information given in the Bible (2 *Kings* iii. 4–27). Apart from this, it is a real piece of literature and indicates that in the ninth century B.C.E. Moab's language and civilization were in general so like the Hebrew that Moabitic can be regarded as a Hebrew dialect.

It would also seem that the Moabite monumental script was closely connected with the Early Hebrew. Nearly all the letters of the Mesha' Stele may be regarded as the connecting link between the letters of the Gezer Calendar and those of the Siloam inscription. We may refer particularly to the letters *beth, kaph, lamed, mem, nun, pe, qoph, shin.*

EARLY MISCELLANEA INSCRIPTIONS

A short inscription discovered in October 1956 in the excavations of the ancient site of Hazor, in Upper Galilee, and assigned by the excavator, Dr. Yigael Yadin, to the eighth century B.C.E., is also in the Early Hebrew monumental style. Its letters resemble those of the Mesha' Stone. Another fragmentary inscription in beautiful Early Hebrew monumental style was discovered in 1936 at Samaria. Only the word *'asher* ("which") is clear, though there are traces of other letters. A few other more or less fragmentary inscriptions are extant, but they do not contribute very much to our knowledge of the Early Hebrew monumental script.

SILOAM INSCRIPTION
Pl. III and VII

Until the discovery of the Gezer Calendar, the Siloam tunnel inscription, casually discovered in June 1880 by some schoolboys, and now preserved in the Museum of Antiquities at Istanbul, was considered the oldest Early Hebrew inscription extant. It is still the main monumental inscription of ancient Israel, though it contains only six lines. It records the labor of those who dug the tunnel. It is now generally agreed that this tunnel is probably that described in the Bible (2 *Kings* xx. 20; 2 *Chr.* xxxii. 3 f. and 30; xxxiii. 14) as having been constructed by King Hezekiah (720–692 B.C.E.). Hence, it is generally assumed that this inscription was cut about 700 B.C.E.

Philologically, the inscription is of very great interest. On the whole, we have here Biblical Hebrew, although there are a few archaic grammatical forms; there is one hitherto unknown word (line 3: *zdh*), which is of uncertain origin. The Siloam inscription is of even greater importance for Epigraphy: the slow but steady development of the Early Hebrew monumental style is clearly evidenced by comparing its letters with those of the Mesha' Stele. For instance, the letters *aleph, waw, zayin, heth,* and *ṣade* are considerably different in the two inscriptions. It may be said that the character of the letters of the Siloam inscription represents the classical Early Hebrew monumental writing; we note particularly the curve of the shafts of the letters *kaph, mem, nun*; the wide and squat form of *zayin* and *ṣade*; the form of the letters *beth, he, waw, lamed, qoph,* and so on.

It is generally known that monumental or lapidary writing, being chiefly employed in engraving on stone, consists of rectilinear letters with angular junctions of the strokes and few if any curves. This angularity is due generally to the type of writing material, mainly stone, but especially to the tool used, which was the chisel. Even a cursory knowledge of the script of Greek or Latin inscriptions, for instance, as compared with the Greek or Latin documents in cursive script, will confirm what has been said with regard to the general character of monumental lettering. But when we examine the Siloam inscription we see quite a different picture: the majority of the letters, and particularly the *kaph*, the *mem*, the

69

nun, have features peculiar to cursive writing (especially the curve of the main shafts) rather than monumental.

In other words, even the Early Hebrew monumental writing is cursive or at any rate is strongly influenced by the cursive script. May we not thus assume that ancient Israel had a very strong tradition of the cursive or literary hand and hardly any tradition of a monumental style? Such a supposition, if it could be proved, would be of paramount importance for enabling us to improve our understanding of the civilization of ancient Israel and of the composition of the Bible.

MINOR SILWÂN INSCRIPTIONS

To the East of Jerusalem, in the neighborhood of the Arab village of Silwân, not far from the Siloam tunnel, several fragmentary funeral inscriptions have been discovered, some containing only one or two words. Some scholars have suggested that the tombs of the Kings of Judah were located here. The inscriptions could therefore have had considerable historical importance. Unfortunately they are in so fragmentary a condition or so poor a state of preservation—only a few words here and there have been deciphered—that their historical value is uncertain. One inscription, in beautiful lettering, has, however, recently been deciphered, as the sepulchral epigraph of Hezekiah's scribe.

JAR-HANDLE STAMPS

One of the most important, and certainly the most numerous, groups of short inscriptions in the Early Hebrew alphabet, is that of the jar-handle stamps, already referred to on p. 58 f. Several hundreds of jar-handles bearing impressions of factory stamps or seals have been found on various sites in southern Israel. Some of these sealings were apparently "royal" trade-marks; others contain what seem to be names of private owners of pottery works, while others—belonging to a later period—are perhaps sealings of the local government of Judaea (*Yehud*); still others are "Jerusalem" stamps or contain other place names. The letters of all these inscriptions, we may assume, are in monumental writing.

About 550 "royal" jar-handle stamps are known. Of all the excavated sites of the Holy Land, Tell ed-Duweir, some twenty-five miles south-west of Jerusalem as the crow flies, the site of the ancient Lachish, produced by far the most remarkable collection; indeed, as many as 325 specimens were discovered there in the years 1935–38. No complete jar containing impressions of sealings has ever been found, but the excavators of Lachish have been able to repair two jars, one bearing four "royal" stamps, the same sealing being stamped on each of the four handles, and the other bears a private stamp. The jar is ovoid, and the potting extremely skilful; its capacity to the base is 9.969 Imperial Standard Gallons or 45.33 litres.

It is interesting to note that the surface of some of the "royal" jar-handles has been blackened by fire; this would no doubt be a result of the fire which destroyed many Hebrew cities when the Babylonians fell upon Judah in 597 or 587 B.C.E. just before they launched their final attack which ended in the fall of Jerusalem, though the possibility of earlier conflagrations cannot be ruled out.

The symbol is of two kinds: (a) a four-winged symbol representing the ordinary Egyptian flying scarab or beetle; and (b) a two-winged figure which may represent a flying or winged scroll—perhaps recalling the still obscure Biblical expression *megillah 'aphah*, "flying roll", in *Zech.* 1 f.—or a bird. Moreover, the four-winged figure may be divided into two classes; in one the figure is treated more naturally, with greater detail in execution; in the second class, the symbol appears more conventionalized. Thus, there are three classes: (1) naturalistic flying scarab; (2) stylized flying scarab; and (3) two-winged figure. These three typological classes correspond to three classes based on epigraphic characteristics.

The three epigraphic classes are so clear that a complete specimen of class (1), or class (2), and of class (3) may serve as typical of the evolution of Early Hebrew monumental writing. In class (1) all the letters are long and thin, and irregular. In class (2) they are generally more squat, wider and shorter, and much more accurate and regular; the main stems of the letters *lamed, mem, nun*, and *pe* are curved and rounded at the bottom; in the *heth* the vertical strokes go beyond the horizontal ones. The letters of class (2) may be regarded as typical representatives of the classical Early Hebrew alphabet. Class (3) shows still further development. Particularly interesting is the *waw* in the Sokoh stamps, consisting of a vertical

71

stem which at the top is curved towards the left and is cut by a hook; the *waw* is followed by an elegant ligature between *kaph* and *he*. In the majority of cases each word is followed by a dot.

The dating of the "royal" jar-handle stamps has been a matter of discussion. Widely different dates have been suggested, ranging from the fourteenth century B.C.E. to the beginning of the Christian era. Nowadays, thanks to the epigraphic evidence, we are able to date these objects, and they in their turn help us to date archaeological sites.

The dating of the three classes of the "royal" stamps is based mainly on a comparison of the styles of writing employed with that in the Siloam inscription. Although on the whole it is dangerous to compare inscriptions of different styles, we can regard the "royal" stamps and the Siloam inscription as belonging to the same class.

In the opinion of the present writer, there is nothing more instructive in the history of the Early Hebrew writing than a comparison between the individual letters of the various types of the "royal" stamps and those of the Siloam inscription, the latter occupying an intermediate position between class (1) and class (2), thus enabling us to consider class (3) a further development of the Early Hebrew monumental script.

The order of development appears so clear that the present writer would not hesitate to assign the introduction of class (1) to a period preceding the Siloam inscription, i.e. to the eighth century B.C.E.; the introduction of class (2) to a period slightly later than the Siloam inscription, i.e. to the seventh century; and the introduction of class (3) to a later period, i.e. to the end of the seventh century B.C.E.

Moreover, there is also the possibility that the change of the four-winged symbol to the two-winged figure was due to Josiah (639–08 B.C.E.), the great religious reformer, who in his determination to stamp out all pagan cults and symbols and to free his country from all foreign influence, may have ordered a change in the official seal of the royal potteries. If this theory is correct the pagan Egyptian scarabaeus was replaced by a bird or the winged Scroll of the Law: 2 *Kings* xxii. 8 and 2 *Chr.* xxxiv. 15 inform us of the discovery of a Law Scroll during repairs to the Temple—a discovery which led to Josiah's drastic religious reforms.

SEALS AND WEIGHTS

The Early Hebrew monumental style can also be studied on seals and weights (see p. 59 f.). After the jar-handle stamps, inscribed seals constitute the most important groups of short Early Hebrew inscriptions. It would seem that about 150 of them are still extant. Over one hundred signet-rings were published in 1934 by the present writer in his collection of Early Hebrew inscriptions. Since then more have been published in various Palestinian, American, Continental, and English journals. More recently other publications have appeared dealing with Early Hebrew seals, and in 1950 the late Prof. A. Reifenberg published a selected collection of about 50 seals.

To judge from *Gen.* xxxviii. 18; 1 *Kings* xxi. 8; *Isaiah* viii. 16 and xxix. 11; *Jer.* xxxii. 10 ff., seals were frequently used in ancient Israel. The earliest inscribed Early Hebrew seals extant belong to the ninth or eighth century B.C.E.; the latest may be attributed to the fourth century B.C.E. The seals show a great variety in shape, though they are mainly oval or scaraboid (the back being slightly vaulted). They were made either of semiprecious hard stones or, though rarely, of soft material such as steatite. The fact that some were made of limestone suggests that seals were also widely used among the common people.

The seals are of great interest both for their inscriptions and their representations. The latter, particularly frequent before the seventh century B.C.E., included "cherubim" and "seraphim" (see *Gen.* iii. 24; *Exod.* xxv. 20; 1 *Sam.* iv. 4 and xxii. 11, and many other passages) and various Egyptian mythological motifs and animals, lions, serpents, scenes of adoration, and so forth. Several seals are veritable works of art. The majority of the seventh and sixth-century B.C.E. seals bear an inscription only and no pictorial representation: this was probably mainly due to the increasing application of the Mosaic prescriptions following the reforms of King Josiah already referred to.

Hardly less important are the seal-inscriptions, which include the names of the owner of these signet-rings. Some seals contain only the name of the owner, others also the patronymicon with or without the word *ben* ("son"). Several of the signets belonged to women, which shows the juridical and social status of women in general. The names, the majority of which contain the *Tetragrammaton*, generally abbreviated, not only increase our knowledge of Early Hebrew nomenclature, but also give us a deep insight into the religious belief of the period to which they belong.

From the point of view of the history of Early Hebrew writing, however, the seals are not of outstanding importance, the seal being primarily an object of art or craftsmanship, though several furnish excellent examples of calligraphy.

EARLY COINS

The few Hebrew coins of the fifth and fourth centuries B.C.E. which have been preserved provide a connecting link between the Early Hebrew monumental writing of the pre-exilic period on the one hand, and on the other, the Jewish coin-script of the Maccabaean period (from 135 B.C.E.), and of the Bar Kochba war (132–5 C.E.), and also the Samaritan script; see also p. 86. Unless we regard the Jewish coin-script and the Samaritan monumental writing (see also p. 91 ff.) as a direct continuation of the Early Hebrew monumental style of writing, the fifth- and fourth-century B.C.E. coins mark the last stage in its history.

CHAPTER 3

CURSIVE SCRIPT

IN CURSIVE AND particularly in current writing the chief consideration is speed and utility. Indeed, the current or running hand naturally assumes a less precise form; the shapes of the letters change quickly, sometimes in the period of a generation: strokes become slurred, angles become more and more curved, superfluities are dropped, and letters are linked together. Individuals develop a personal handwriting.

Changes in the current hand no doubt tend to arise from a natural indolence or inertia on the part of individual scribes. In addition, the natural or individual hand of the scribe would also tend to assert itself; and current shapes begin to make their appearance intermingled with the more formal characters. In the course of time, with the current hand the writing often degenerates until it is superseded by a reformed style, which in its turn runs its course.

SAMARIAN OSTRACA

The Samarian ostraca—ostraca being documents written in ink on potsherds, pieces of a broken jar—are the earliest extant documents written in the Early Hebrew current or running hand. About eighty of them were discovered in 1910 at Sebastiye, the ancient Samaria. On epigraphical grounds the writing could be ascribed to the ninth or eighth century B.C.E., but on archaeological grounds the Samarian ostraca are now commonly assigned to the early eighth century B.C.E. It would seem, however, that they could as easily date from the last years of the reign of Jehoahaz, that is the end of the ninth century.

In contrast with the monumental style, the Samarian ostraca point to the practice of a cursive style and the use of a reed-pen. This beautiful current hand differs so significantly from the lapidary style of the Siloam inscription that the two styles can hardly be considered to belong to the same line of evolution. For instance, the letter *mem* of Siloam seems to have been written with four strokes, while the *mem* of the Samarian ostraca was written with one stroke of the pen. As the script of the Samarian ostraca already shows a lengthy process of evolution, we may suppose that an independent cursive style had long been in use in ancient Israel, and that it was probably used both for literary and for everyday purposes.

Interestingly enough from the chronological point of view the Siloam inscription is supposed to be far more advanced than the Samarian ostraca. Some letters of the latter show a more archaic form than those of the former; for instance, the *daleth* in the Samarian ostraca has hardly any tail; the *zayin* is less squat than that in the Siloam inscription; the shafts in the letters *kaph*, *mem*, and *nun* are less curved than those in the Siloam inscription. Yet, because of the cursive style, the letters *beth*, *he*, *yodh*, *pe*, *ṣade*, *qoph*, and *resh* in the Samarian ostraca are more evolved than those of Siloam.

LACHISH LETTERS
Pl. III and VIII

The cursive style reached its climax in the Lachish Letters of the beginning of the sixth century B.C.E. The twenty-one documents are probably a very small remnant of a large correspondence and of a cache of other written documents. Indeed, hundreds of other jar fragments were found there, but owing to their burnt and decayed condition, it is impossible to say whether they had once been inscribed. Moreover, only a small part of Lachish has been excavated and numerous other documents may still be buried at this site. Nevertheless, it has been rightly remarked that these documents, very imperfect though they are, bring us into close contact with the inner religious, political, and military life of the Kingdom of Judah perhaps in the last year of its independence.

The Lachish ostraca are all written in iron-carbon ink, apparently with a reed or wood-pen; the nib part must have been broad but not thick. The script is a fluent cursive, and appears to have been the work of scribes well accustomed to such writing. This script makes us realize, as indeed a scholar has pointed out, that the ancient Israelites could write quickly and boldly, in an artistic flowing hand, with the loving penmanship of those who enjoy writing.

The Lachish Letters bear a striking resemblance in many respects—writing material, current hand, etc.—to the Samarian ostraca, and we can usefully compare the current script employed respectively in the early sixth century B.C.E. and about 800 B.C.E. Nearly all the letters in the Lachish ostraca show cursive development: it will suffice to draw the reader's attention to the shapes of the *zayin, yodh, kaph, nun, samekh, qoph,* and *resh.*

At the same time, the Lachish ostraca exhibit many characteristics of the current as distinct from the literary hand. Here we may mention that different characteristics are found in the much later *Leviticus* fragments (see further on). It is also interesting to note that some of the Lachish Letters were written hurriedly, for there are many cases of *haplography,* that is, omission, in writing, of one or two consecutive identical letters or groups of letters, as well as mistakes of various kinds, omissions of the dividing dot between words, and so on.

Even more instructive is a comparison between the letters of the Lachish ostraca and those of the Early Hebrew monumental writing. Although hardly any letter in the two styles is sufficiently different to confuse even a layman, the majority of the Lachish-ostraca characters reached their zenith in cursiveness.

OTHER CURRENT-HAND DOCUMENTS

Several other ostraca have come to light. In 1932 five inscribed fragments were found at Samaria. Of these, Ostracon C. 1101 deserves particular mention. It may be attributed to the late ninth or early eighth century B.C.E. Only three lines, partly fragmentary, have been preserved. It appears to be a private letter concerning an agricultural consignment. The main epigraphical feature of the document is the extremely long shape of the letters *lamed, mem* and *nun.* This feature could lead us to assign the document to a relatively early period, probably the ninth century B.C.E. The current characteristics of the inscriptions are most interesting, particularly the curved shafts of the letters *beth, kaph, mem, nun,* and the squat form of the *yodh,* which are features of a slightly later period.

Two interesting eighth-century B.C.E. ostraca were found in 1948 at Tell Qasile, North of Tel Aviv. One of them, mentioning gold from Ophir (1 *Kings* ix. 28; xxii. 49), is particularly interesting, not least because of its ligatures. Another eighth-century current-hand inscription was discovered in 1956 at Hazor. Of slightly later date (late eighth or early seventh century B.C.E.) is a fragmentary ostracon from Tell en-Naṣbe, the site of ancient Miṣpah. Its main interest lies in the fact that it contains, what appears to be, a foreign name. The letters are of rather unusual form, which may indicate a foreign scribe.

The peculiar forms of some of the letters of the Ophel Ostracon, found in 1924, which is generally assigned to the seventh century B.C.E., are of interest. The *waw*, *yodh*, *nun*, *qoph* are especially noteworthy.

NUMERICAL NOTATION

Not much can be added with regard to numerical figures: in the Samarian ostraca there are symbols for the numbers 1, 2, 15 and 17; the number 30 occurs in the Tell Qasile ostracon. Otherwise, apart from some uncertain symbols on weights, the numbers are usually expressed by words.

CHAPTER 4

EARLY HEBREW LITERARY HAND

THE *Leviticus* AND other small Early Hebrew fragments recently found in the Dead Sea caves together with the by-now-famous Dead Sea Scrolls (see p. 144 ff.), are the only remains of what we consider to be the Early Hebrew book- or literary hand. There are five fragments from *Leviticus* (xix. 31–34; xx. 20–23; xxi. 24–xxii. 3; xxii. 4–5), and they agree astonishingly with the Massoretic Text, except for *Lev.* xx. 21, where significantly enough the word *niddah* is written with *yodh* and not *waw*, thus supporting the *qerì* of the Massoretic Text.

EMPLOYMENT OF PAPYRUS AND LEATHER

From the Lachish ostraca we realize (see p. 76) that the Hebrew contemporaries of Jeremiah could write quickly and boldly in an artistic flowing hand. In all probability—it has been rightly suggested—Jeremiah himself would have used this script when he subscribed the deed relating to the purchase of the field at Anathoth, and so too would the witnesses to the deed (*Jer.* xxxii. 6 ff.), and Baruch also would have written in this script at Jeremiah's dictation "upon a roll of a book" (*Jer.* xxxvi. 4, cf. also 32). The roll was probably of papyrus. The clay impressions referred to on p. 56 attest to the use of papyrus as writing material. Incidental as well as direct confirmation of the frequent use of rolls of papyrus or parchment is found in the Bible: *Jer.* xxxvi. 4 has been mentioned above; *Isaiah*, xxix. 11 f. refers either to papyrus or to parchment; and *Ezek.* ii. 9 f. probably refers to skin as writing material; see also *Zech.* v. 1 and *Psalm* ci. 8.

At any rate, there can be no doubt that Early Hebrew book-production goes back to very early times. The *Book of Esther* is known in Hebrew as *megillath-Esther*, and the *Five Megilloth* indicate the books of *Esther, Canticles, Ruth, Lamentations,* and *Ecclesiastes*, but the Hebrew word *megillah* means "roll", and only papyrus, parchment or leather could form book-rolls. The *Talmud* regulation that all copies of the *Torah* must be

79

written on rolls (or scrolls) of skin probably reflects a much earlier tradition. Thanks to this regulation, which is still in force, there exist many thousands of such Law Scrolls all over the world. *Exod.* xxvi. 14 shows that the art of preparing and coloring skins was known in very early times. *Num.* v. 23 would seem to refer to a leather-scroll—"And the priest shall write these curses in a scroll, and he shall blot them out into the water of bitterness"—since it is rather difficult to erase writing from papyrus. *Ezek.* ii. 9 f., already referred to, is of particular significance: this mentions a roll written *panîm ve-aḥor*, that is "on both sides", and no doubt it suggests leather rather than any other writing material.

Further evidence of the use of leather or parchment for the Hebrew *Torah* Scrolls is provided by the "letter" of Pseudo-Aristeas, which nowadays is assigned to the middle of the second century B.C.E. This "letter" refers to a magnificent copy of the *Torah* written on *diphtherai*, that is leather, in letters of gold, which was supposed to have been sent to King Ptolemy I of Egypt in 285 B.C.E. for the purpose of making the *Septuagint*.

[The *Letter of Aristeas* is a small Greek literary work, which purports to be a letter written by Aristeas, an official of Ptolemy II Philadelphus (King of Egypt, 285–245 B.C.E.) to his brother Philocrates giving him an account of the translation of the Pentateuch in Greek, i.e. the *Septuagint*. In reality, the details of the narrative are, in the main, fictitious, and the work seems to have been a piece of Jewish apologetic literature of the Ptolemaic period.]

To sum up, it is most probable that from very early times costly leather was the regular material for formal copies of books or for important or official documents, while the much cheaper papyrus, together with the ostraca, discussed earlier, was employed for cheaper kinds of books, and for more or less private and merely ephemeral matters. Moreover, it is at least probable that such books of leather or papyrus were written not in a monumental style or in a current hand, but in a literary or book-hand. A book-hand may have been employed by the secretaries of the kings of ancient Israel and of the prophets.

As no remains of pre-Exilic books written in such a hand have so far come to light, nothing can be said about its origin and development, but it is hardly to be assumed that the original book-hand—and there may well have been various literary-hands—could have differed from the original current hand. Indeed, not only are mutual influences to be expected even during the period of its development, but, as in the case of any other cultured nation, schools and other means of instruction must have had some effect on it.

SIGNIFICANCE OF THE DEAD-SEA EARLY-HEBREW FRAGMENTS

The *Leviticus* as well as the other Early Hebrew fragments found in the Dead Sea caves are written with ink on leather, and are unique from the point of view of palaeography. The majority of the preserved letters are clear and neat, and in the opinion of the present writer there can be no doubt that this script represents a beautiful Early Hebrew literary-hand, the first of its kind ever discovered.

It is interesting to note that the words are always separated by dots or short strokes, as in the Siloam inscription, the Samaria ostraca, some parts of the Lachish Letters, some Early Hebrew jar-handle stamps and seals, the Samaritan, and the early Phoenician and Aramaic inscriptions. The end of Chapter xxi of *Leviticus* is marked by a blank space.

THEIR DATING

The dating of the present fragments is extremely difficult, for three reasons. First, the fragments themselves do not provide any direct evidence for dating. Second, there are no contemporary written documents with which they can properly be compared. Third, we are probably dealing with a standardized literary hand which was used, perhaps only with slight alterations, for centuries. The last reason may perhaps explain why some of the letters of the Dead Sea fragments appear in what may seem an earlier form than that of the letters of the Lachish ostraca, written in a sixth-century B.C.E. current hand, and why, therefore, some scholars at first considered these fragments contemporary with the Lachish documents.

If we bear in mind the main characteristics of the Early Hebrew alphabet, we realize that some of these are rather accentuated in the Dead Sea fragments. We can refer, for example, to the squat, wide, and short forms of the letters *beth*,

81

mem, yodh, kaph, ṣade, and *resh*; the curved tails of *beth, kaph, mem* and *nun*; the wide heads and tails of *kaph* and *mem*; the oblique shape of *he* and *yodh*, and so on. The forms of the letters *aleph, beth, yodh, kaph, mem, nun,* and *ṣade* in particular may be regarded as transitional between the classical Early Hebrew script and those of the early Samaritan alphabet and of the Jewish coin-script, due allowance being made for the different styles of the particular documents.

A detailed examination of the single letters of the new fragments and a comparison with the early Samaritan alphabet and the Jewish coin-script—but particularly with the former—induces us to assign them, at least provisionally, to the late fourth or the early third century B.C.E. On the other hand, their presence amongst the other Dead Sea Scrolls shows that the Early Hebrew alphabet was still known in the first pre-Christian century or the first century C.E. The use of the Early Hebrew writing on the Jewish coins is decisive evidence that the Early Hebrew alphabet lingered on as late as the second century C.E., although in a rather stylized form.

THE TETRAGRAMMATON

The "lingering on" of the Early Hebrew literary hand in the early Christian centuries is substantiated by Christian literary sources. Origen (186–c. 254) and Jerome (*d.* 420) mention that in "accurate manuscripts" the *Tetragrammaton* (*YHWH* = the Hebrew name of God) was written in Early Hebrew letters. The *Tetragrammaton* had, of course, a unique significance, not only for the ancient and medieval Jew but also for the early Christians. Hence, very early Greek copies of the Bible have preserved the *Tetragrammaton* in the Early Hebrew script, though in so stylized a form that it looked, and was read, as if it were the Greek word ΠΙΠΙ. A document as late as the sixth-century C.E. uncial palimpsest of Aquila's Greek translation of 2 *Kings*, still contains such a form.

One of the Dead Sea MSS., the *Habakkuk Commentary*, proves the correctness of Origen's statement for Hebrew manuscripts. The *Habakkuk Commentary* is written in the Square Hebrew script, but the *Tetragrammaton* is in Early Hebrew. The stylized and rather unusual forms of the letters, however, show not only that they were written by a scribe who had no experience of Early Hebrew script, but also that on the whole the old script had become increasingly less familiar. On the other hand, other Square Hebrew fragments found in the same cave contain the word *'el* (= "God") written in Early Hebrew letters of a late, but non-stylized type, which shows that their scribe had some familiarity with this script.

NOTARIQON (?)

Some of the Dead Sea manuscripts, such as the Scroll *Isaiah A*, the *Habakkuk Commentary*, and the *Sectarian Document*, contain marginal markings and other curious-looking symbols. Their origin and meaning are still uncertain, though various interpretations have been suggested. At any rate, in the majority of cases they resemble Early Hebrew letters, either single or double, and are extremely cursive though very stylized. Easily recognizable are the letters *waw*, *zayin*, *samekh*, *'ayin*, *ṣade*, *taw*.

If there is any connection between these symbols and the Early Hebrew alphabet, it would explain why in a Jewish tradition, transmitted in *Tanchuma: Wayyesheb*, ii, and *Pirkê-de R. Eliezer*, xxxviii, this script was also known as *notariqon*, that is a notary's or stenographer's script, or else, a documentary script. On this basis Prof. Montgomery (*The Samaritans*, p. 283), thinks that the Early Hebrew alphabet was much better fitted for rapid writing than the Square Hebrew, and may have survived in business use till a comparatively late period.

EMPLOYMENT OF THE EARLY HEBREW ALPHABET IN POST-EXILIC TIMES

It is obviously a matter of opinion whether the Early Hebrew or the Square Hebrew script was better fitted for rapid writing. If the former, this would show not only that the Early Hebrew alphabet was still known in the first Christian centuries, but that it was in frequent use and could be speedily written. It is, however, more likely that some Early Hebrew words or letters or compounds of letters became as it were fossil remains or "ideograms" similar to the Aramaic "ideograms" in the Pahlavi script or Latin "ideograms" in English, such as *d.*, £, *et*, *e.g.*, *i.e.*, *viz.*, and many others. However that may be, there can be no doubt that the Early Hebrew alphabet must have survived in odd cases for many centuries after it had ceased to be general. Indeed, the employment of the Early Hebrew alphabet in post-exilic times is explicitly or implicitly indicated in several literary sources and even in Mishnaic tradition.

JEWISH LITERARY SOURCES

The author of the *Book of Esther* (viii. 9) makes it clear that the Jews of that time had their own script and their own language. This script could hardly have been the Aramaic script, which was in use throughout the whole Near East, especially in Persia; indeed, it was an official script of the Empire. It was certainly not peculiar to the Jews.

In *Yadaim*, iv. 5 we read:

> "The (Aramaic) version that is in Ezra and Daniel renders the hands unclean. If an (Aramaic) version (contained in the Scriptures) was written in Hebrew, or if (Scripture that is in) Hebrew was written in an (Aramaic) version, or in Hebrew script, it does not render the hands unclean. (The Holy Scriptures) render the hands unclean only if they are written in the Assyrian character, on leather, and in ink." (For the meaning of the term "unclean" see p. 132.)

Similar evidence is also provided by *Baraitha Shabbath*, 115*b*, and other Talmudic passages. This tradition should be taken to mean that the Square Hebrew alphabet became *the* Holy script of the Jews, but we may assume that the Early Hebrew character was still in use even for religious purposes.

Prof. Tur-Sinai raises some interesting questions: why the use in the Talmudic sources of obscure terms for a script which was still in use in the days of the Tannaim, as evidenced by the Bar Kochba coins? How could Rabbi El'azar of Modin, a contemporary of Bar Kochba, have implied that the *Torah* was originally written in "Assyrian" and not in the "Hebrew" script? How could Rabbi Judah ha-Nasi have held the same view, adding furthermore that the change from the original "Assyrian" to the Early Hebrew script was intended as a punishment for sins? Why, indeed, should this change in script be regarded as a punishment?

We shall try to find an answer to all these problems below, but in Prof. Tur-Sinai's opinion, their solution lies in a new interpretation of the term *ketabh*; according to him this does not mean "script", but "book" or "text", and the terms

84

'*ashshurî* and '*ibhri* would be basically geographical terms, only later having acquired linguistic connotations.

Thus, *ketabh 'ashshurî* would indicate the *Torah*—text employed in Assyria—a term covering all the countries in the Mediterranean area inhabited by "Aramaeans", while *ketabh 'ibhrî* would apply only to the Palestinian text. Thus, the issue would be the primacy of the text brought by Ezra from Babylonia, the only authentic text, as against the Samaritan text employed in Palestine which, according to Judah ha-Nasi, would be *da'aṣ*, meaning a stick without roots and vitality planted in the soil, instead of a living plant, or according to other rabbis *ketabh libona'ah*, "a false" or "spurious" text.

Tur-Sinai's assumption that *ketabh* is never used in the Talmud with the meaning of "script" is not correct, and his suggestions that it should be interpreted as "book" or "text", that the *ketabh 'ibhrî* or *ketabh libona'ah*, having been the original text, should be interpreted as a "false" or "spurious" text, are inconceivable. Also the term '*ibhrî* cannot but mean the Hebrew language. For instance, in *Sifrê, Comment. on Deut. xxxiii.* 2, we read that God revealed Himself to Israel through the *Torah* in four languages, *lashon 'ibhrî, lashon romî, lashon 'arabî,* and *lashon 'aramî*: it is only obvious that the first of these four is the "Hebrew language".

CHRISTIAN TRADITION

The Fathers of the Church (who mainly depended on Jewish sources for their information) have more or less the same tradition. We have referred to Origen and Jerome in connection with the *Tetragrammaton*. From what Origen writes it may be inferred that the Early Hebrew script was still known not many generations before his own time. Epiphanius (315–403) upholds the tradition that there was no break between the Early Hebrew script and the Samaritan script, and it is perhaps also possible to infer from his words that the Samaritans were not the only people who continued to employ the Early Hebrew script.

PSEUDO-ARISTEAS

Apart from the Talmudic tradition and that of the Church Fathers, indirect evidence is provided by the second-century B.C.E. "letter" of Pseudo-Aristeas (see p. 80). This work mentions "the peculiar characters of the Jews"; and it is

85

highly probable that it refers to the Early Hebrew script, and not the Aramaic, which was well known to the Egyptians.

EARLIEST PRESERVED COINS

In discussing the problem of the use of the Early Hebrew alphabet in post-exilic times, we must also deal with the extant coins of the fifth and fourth centuries B.C.E., which were referred to on p. 74. These early coins contain the words *Yehud*, "Judaea"—probably indicating the small semi-autonomous state of Judaea under Persian sovereignty; *beqa'*, the name of a weight (see p. 59) and later of a coin; and also the name *Hezekiah*.

While nearly all the letters of these coins show a more or less transitional form, it is particularly interesting to examine more closely the form of *qoph* in *beqa'*. The late Prof. Reifenberg, who did not regard the Jewish coin-script as a direct continuation of the Early Hebrew writing, wrote: "Although somewhat similar forms of *qoph* do occur on earlier inscriptions, the letter employed here resembles most closely the archaistic writing on the late Hebrew shekels and may represent a transitional form between the old Hebrew and the shekel characters. We see, therefore, that the script is well in line with the chronological classification arrived at on the basis of stylistic features."

CHAPTER 5

JEWISH COIN-ALPHABET AND SAMARITAN SCRIPT

Pl. IX–X

MANY LEADING SCHOLARS still hold that the script used on the Jewish coins from the Maccabaean age to Bar Kochba's revolt (*c.* 135 B.C.E.–135 C.E.) and the Samaritan script, which is still used for liturgical purposes by the Samaritans, the remainder of the ancient Jewish sect, numbering today only a few hundred, were artificially revived some centuries after the Early Hebrew alphabet had fallen into disuse. Indeed, in the opinion for instance of Prof. W. F. Albright, the foremost expert on Palestinian archaeology, "the revival of pre-exilic script in Maccabaean coins . . . was purely archaizing and does not represent a continued evolution of the current script." Moreover, "it would be only natural to date the final schism between" the Jews and the Samaritans "somewhere in the early first century B.C. It was presumably then that the entire Samaritan Pentateuch was retranscribed into the archaizing 'Samaritan' script, which symbolized the refusal of the Samaritans to follow the 'modernists' of Jerusalem."

However, in the opinion of the present writer it is hardly likely that an obsolete script would have been taken out of the drawer, so to speak, and chosen for objects such as coins, which are in general use. Moreover, assuming that the Square Hebrew alphabet was the only script known and employed by the population of the Hasmonaean state, what mysterious reasons would have induced its rulers to revive a long forgotten script? On the other hand, if the Square Hebrew script was too sacred to be used for secular purposes, was not the Hebrew language even more sacred?

Analogous common-sense objections may be made with regard to the origin of the Samaritan script. But there is more to it. The difference between the Samaritan script and the Aramaic writing adopted by the Jews in post-exilic times was claimed by the Samaritans as proof of the priority of their own,

87

and became a subject of dispute in the polemics of the two hostile parties, especially as not only the Samaritans but also the Jews call the older script which the Samaritans preserved *ketabh 'ibrî*, "the Hebrew script". According to Jewish tradition (see p. 127) the "Hebrew script was left" to the Samaritans. Is it at all possible that in the sharp Judaeo-Samaritan polemics any Jewish controversialist would have failed to point out—if there was any sure basis for the suggestion—that only in quite recent times (about the first century B.C.E.) the Samaritans retranscribed their Pentateuch in an out-of-date script? (See also p. 92f.)

JEWISH COIN-ALPHABET

Pl. IX

We can hardly understand why the Jewish coin-script was used unless we appreciate the internal situation of the early Hasmonaean state and its international background. A leading American scholar, Prof. M. Burrows, has pointed out that in Palestine, and probably only there, there was a strong reaction against the Hellenizing movement, which seemed to conservative Jews to run counter to all the traditions of their fathers and to imperil the ancient heritage of Israel. At the same time, there was conflict between the more aristocratic conservatives, who kept the old Jewish religious beliefs transmitted by the Law and the Prophets, and nothing more, and the popular leaders, representatives of the masses, who took account also of the later traditions and literature. On the whole, however, there was little compromise between Judaism and the ideas of Hellenism which had penetrated the Orient after the victory of Alexander the Great—and only in little Judaea was there any resistance to Hellenism. Still, even in Judaea there was a compromise party, a kind of liberal Judaism in a Hellenized form, as it has been described by one scholar. Indeed, a movement was begun for the reorganization of Judaism as a sort of Syro-Hellenic religion; this finally resulted in the outbreak of the Hasmonaean revolt in 168–7 B.C.E. The revolt against the spread of Hellenism in Judaea succeeded because all pious Jews regardless of party realized that no reconciliation between pagan Hellenistic polytheism and Jewish monotheism was possible. Thus, monotheism was preserved—for the world.

It may be assumed that when finally in 138 B.C.E. Antiochus VII issued a decree (1 *Macc.* xv. 2–9) granting Simon the right to strike Judaean coins, these reflected the national feeling of the time. Simon, we are told, augmented the sacred vessels of the Temple, and apparently proceeded to represent them on the coins, where we find the chalice used for wine-offerings; the *lulabh* and *ethrog*, symbols of the Feast of Tabernacles; a basket full of fruits, apparently an allusion to the offerings of the first-fruits; and, on the other face of the coin, a palm-tree, which was a symbol of the country.

None of these symbols reflects an archaizing tendency, none appears on earlier coins of the country. On the contrary, they all represent living realities, objects known to everybody, and regarded by everybody as religio-national symbols. Is there any reason to suppose that the script chosen for use on these coins was archaizing, an exception to the general rule? If in the second half of the second century B.C.E. the Square Hebrew alphabet were really the only one used in Judaea both for religious and secular purposes, it would be reasonable to assume that this was not only the religious but also the national script. Certainly, in the employment of Square Hebrew there could not have been any suspicion of assimilationist tendencies towards Hellenism.

On the contrary, the past associations of the Early Hebrew script, particularly if this had not been used for the preceding centuries, were undoubtedly more "pagan"—as indicated by the Early Hebrew seals, jar-handle stamps, or even the Judaean fifth- and fourth-century coins—than those of the Square Hebrew script.

COIN-SCRIPT (Pl. IX)

It would therefore seem that the coin-alphabet cannot be considered archaizing. It must have been a script still in use amongst a section of the population. We may go further and say that it must have been considered *the* national script of the Judaeans. The argument that there are not many Early Hebrew inscriptions—and, for that matter, no Square Hebrew inscriptions—which can be assigned to the period of about 400 years between the end of the Judaean monarchy and the Hasmonaean dynasty, cuts both ways. It can be argued either

89

that the Early Hebrew script fell into disuse or that what is considered an archaized form represents in fact a later phase in the evolution of the script.

The arguments that in the coin-script the form of the letters differs in many respects from the script of the pre-exilic documents, and that the characters are in the main stylized, giving the impression that the script is an artificial one, may be discounted. We do not know precisely the stages by which the Early Hebrew monumental script developed prior to the period when the Hasmonaean coins appear. Moreover, differences in the form of letters on the coins may also be due either to the numismatic style or to the idiosyncrasies of engravers. This becomes evident when we compare the styles of the scripts of the various coins. The many irregular features of the coin-script are most typically represented by the inscription "Eleazar the Priest"—which exhibits, in the words of an expert in numismatics, "strange letter-order, omissions, transpositions, abbreviations, parts of letters reversed and whole inscriptions written in 'retrograde' direction, distorted forms, and meaningless surface-scratched characters."

In Mildenberg's opinion, the large number of these irregular forms suggests that even the die-engravers—not to speak of the public—were not fully acquainted with the Early Hebrew script. But the general character of the script is the same. A glance at any table of the Early Hebrew alphabet will show that the Jewish coin-script finds its appropriate place—due consideration being given to the general characteristics of the numismatic style—as a continuation of the Early Hebrew alphabet.

SIGNIFICANCE OF THE COINS

The period of the Second Temple, particularly in the last stages of the heroic war for independence of Rome, is one of the most creative epochs in all Jewish history, but is also the least known. For certain information about the period, the coins are the most valuable if not the only source. Particularly in the matter of dating, the coins—especially those of the Second Jewish War, 132–5 C.E.—tell us a good deal more than can be deduced from literary sources.

Either Simon to whom the right to strike coins was granted in 138 B.C.E. (see p. 89) or John Hyrcanus, 135–104 B.C.E., was the first Jewish ruler actually to issue coins. Alexander

Jannaeus (103–76 B.C.E.) was the first to style himself king on his coins, and to stamp his name and title in Greek also. Herod I (37–4 B.C.E.) was the first Jewish ruler to use only Greek writing on his coins, and Herod Philip II (4 B.C.E.–34 C.E.) the first to use the effigy of the Roman Emperor.

COIN-EMBLEMS (Pl. IX)

With very rare exceptions, only such emblems were used as would not offend religious susceptibilities: cornucopias, flowers, bunches of grapes, anchor, etc. (see also p. 89). The *menorah*, which later became the most characteristic symbol of Judaism, and is now the main part of the State-emblem of Israel, appeared for the first time on the coins of Antigonus Mattathia (40–37 B.C.E.), whose Hebrew name we know only from coins.

Of particular significance are the silver shekels struck during the First Jewish War (66–70 C.E.) which were meant to be used for the payment of Temple-dues. They contain the representation of the chalice on the obverse and the pomegranates on the reverse, the inscriptions being *Sheqel Israel*, with the date, and *Yerushalayim ha-qedoshah* ("Jerusalem the Holy").

In Reifenberg's authoritative opinion, the sovereign Jewish coinage reached its highest standard of workmanship at the very time when the last serious rising was brutally crushed, that is, in 135 C.E. But not only did the modest designs, showing the intensity of national feeling, survive in the synagogue art of the first Christian centuries, but they also influenced Jewish art during the Middle Ages and indeed continue to be used in our own time. Their particular script, however, was forgotten.

The new State of Israel has revived the symbols of the ancient coins, and uses them on its own coins and stamps, imitating the ancient script. Thus, having linked up the end of the ancient independence with its own fresh beginning, modern Israel has also revived the script which was born with the birth of the Hebrew nation (see p. 37 f.).

SAMARITAN SCRIPT
Pl. X

This script also is generally regarded not as a continuation of the Early Hebrew alphabet but as a new, archaizing creation of about the first century B.C.E. (see p. 87). A comparison of the earliest Samaritan inscription extant, the Emmaus-, or al-Amwas, bilingual with the Early Hebrew script on the one hand, and with the Jewish coin-alphabet on the other, would be sufficient to show that the Samaritan script is nothing but a continuation of the Early Hebrew script. It is true that the Emmaus inscription has been regarded by some scholars as Hebrew and not as Samaritan—in fact it may be both—but if it were Hebrew it would provide an even better connecting link between the Early Hebrew and Samaritan scripts. The date of the Emmaus-bilingual is still under discussion; it probably belongs to the last pre-Christian or the first Christian century. However, in the opinion of the present writer it may be considered a specimen of the last stage of the Early Hebrew monumental script.

ORIGIN OF SAMARITAN SCRIPT

Prof. Albright has pointed out that the characters of the Emmaus inscription resemble those of the enigmatic Jewish coins of the "fourth year" (referred to on p. 190) more closely than they do those of any other known script, and that other early Samaritan letters, not found in this inscription, also closely resemble the characters on these coins. Unfortunately, the date of the coins is also debatable. However, in Albright's opinion, this interesting similarity of script presumably means that the designers of these coins followed the same epigraphic tradition as that employed by the Samaritans who carved the Emmaus bilingual. This suggestion is corroborated by other evidence, and thus there can be no doubt that the early "Samaritan" script is closely related to the Jewish coin-alphabet. It would thus appear that the solution of the problem of origin in the one case should facilitate the solution of the same problem in the other.

It is highly probable that the Samaritan script, like the Jewish coin-script (see p. 88 ff.), was a direct continuation of the Early Hebrew alphabet. The suggestion referred to on p. 87 that the entire Samaritan Pentateuch was retranscribed into the "archaizing" Samaritan script does not accord with Jewish tradition: see p. 127. The Talmud gives no indication whatever of the existence of a Jewish tradition on the subject. This, however, is one of those rare cases where negative evidence is good evidence: the polemics about the priority of the Bible of the Jews over that of the Samaritans might reasonably be

92

expected to contain some taunt that the hated and "contemptible" sect retranscribed their Bible at a later period (see also p. 87).

The situation with regard to script probably corresponded to that regarding language. In the opinion of Prof. Z. Ben-Hayyim, the Israeli authority on the Samaritans, "the term 'Samaritan Tradition' is merely conventional. Actually we are dealing here with a linguistic entity formerly diffused amongst Jews beyond the confines of the Samaritan community. ... The idea, entertained a hundred years ago, that the Samaritans picked their form of language out of a spirit of religious and spiritual opposition to their Jewish rivals, seemed even then somewhat far-fetched."

It may be assumed that until the third century C.E. the Samaritans used the Early Hebrew alphabet, as it was employed by some other sections of the Jewish nation. Although the Samaritans took no part in the immortal struggle of their Jewish brethren against the Syrians, they played some part in the First Jewish War, and they also participated in the Bar Kochba war. After the destruction of Jewish political hopes under Hadrian (135 C.E.), however, the Pharisaic party won the upper hand. The discussions went on during the second and third centuries. Such influential men as R. Akiba, R. Meir, and R. Simeon b. Gamaliel still favored a tolerant line towards the Samaritans. But eventually the Samaritans were put on the same level as the Gentiles and about 300 C.E. the hated sect was excommunicated.

DEVELOPMENT OF SAMARITAN SCRIPT

It would seem that the Samaritan alphabet did not achieve "independence" until the third century C.E. This "independence" coincided with a Samaritan religious revival and reformation, which was instituted by a man known as Baba Rabba, assigned by Samaritan tradition to the third or fourth century C.E.

Although Samaritan epigraphy at first sight gives the impression of standardization, closer examination reveals that it gradually underwent certain modifications which reflect changes in scribal style with the passing of generations. Prof. W. R. Taylor refers to the alteration of the ancient letters by the introduction of diacritical lines; the introduction of the colon and of the colon with a dash, to mark respectively the

93

end of a sentence and of a section, in addition to the ancient dot as a word divider; the use of shading in the strokes, of flourishes and of knots for calligraphic ends, etc. In Taylor's opinion, these and other changes are steps in the evolution of a rabbinical script; indeed, Taylor sees an inter-relation between the Samaritan script and the Square Hebrew.

A discussion of the development of the Samaritan script— so far as we can speak of such development—is beyond the limits of the present book. It will suffice to conclude that if our theory of the origin of the Samaritan script be accepted, this script, with its three styles, would be the only offshoot of the Early Hebrew alphabet still in use, although only for liturgical purposes.

LINK-UP WITH THE EARLY HEBREW ALPHABET

Assuming that the Jewish coin-script and the Samaritan script are direct descendants of the Early Hebrew alphabet, how did the alphabet itself come to be kept alive between the Babylonian exile and the Hasmonaean national revival, a period of nearly $4\frac{1}{2}$ centuries?

It may be suggested that it continued to be used by those who were not exiled. The Aramaic alphabet, introduced from Mesopotamia into Palestine perhaps as early as the late Assyrian or in the neo-Babylonian period, and was certainly in use in the Persian period, was not at first popular amongst the people of Palestine, attached as they were to their ancient religion and culture. With the return of the Judeaean exiles in the days of Ezra—if we are to accept Jewish tradition as preserved in *Sanhedrin* 21*b* (see Part III)—pre-eminence was given to the new script in religious circles. The *Torah* and other sacred books were re-written in *ketabh 'ashshurî* ("Assyrian" characters). Certain sections of the population, however, such as the *hedyoṭoth*—probably the Sadducees, the *'am ha-areṣ*, and the Samaritans—continued to employ the old script even for the Holy Scriptures. They were all disliked by the Pharisees, from whom they differed in a more or less identical way as we can see, for instance, from *Ḥagigah* ii. 7; *Berakh.* 47*b*; *Yadaim* iv. 5; *Niddah* iv. 2; *Menaḥoth* 42*b*; *Pessaḥ* 49*b*, etc.

At the same time, we can understand the peculiar hostility

of the Pharisees towards the old script when we realize that they regarded the Early Hebrew writing as a punishment for Israel's sins (see also p. 128): see *Tosefta Sanh.* iv. 7. May we not therefore assume that the Sadducees, the *'am ha-ares*, and the Samaritans considered it the national script? Indeed, the Pharisees themselves in effect admitted as much when they called the script *ketabh 'ibhri*, "the Hebrew writing".

HASMONAEANS—PHARISEES—SADDUCEES

The Hasmonaeans owed their miraculous success very largely to having unified the various factions in the struggle for political and religious independence: they had the support of the worldly, aristocratic party of the Sadducees and of the religiously puritan party of the Pharisees. The descendants of the Babylonian exiles and their disciples were originally the main bulk of the party out of which the Pharisees grew. In their passionate desire to keep afloat the Jewish ship in the Hellenistic ocean, the Pharisees wholeheartedly supported the Hasmonaean cause.

When the Hasmonaean revolt had resulted in victory, both parties were upholders of the *Torah* and of political independence, but in the course of time the "*Torah* party" became chiefly concerned in upholding the *Torah* in its purity and in guarding it from the intrusion of worldly considerations. But the increasing worldliness of the Priest-kings began in the course of time to alienate their most important Pharisaic friends. The rift between the two parties gradually widened, until the two main sects appeared, the Sadducees and the Pharisees, the paramount difference between them being that the former denied the validity of the Oral Law, which the latter upheld. It was towards the end of John Hyrcanus' reign (135–104 B.C.E.) that a series of events occurred which transformed the Pharisaic movement into a religio-political party of the opposition prepared to defend their rights at all costs.

It was the party of the Sadducees which mainly influenced the dynasty of the Hasmonaeans, at first unofficially and later officially. Indeed, the Sadducees and the Hasmonaeans seem constantly to have drawn closer together. As a consequence, when the question arose of the script to be used for the new coins, the Maccabees preferred the advice given to them by the Sadducees and selected as their coin-script the Early Hebrew alphabet, i.e., the national script, which was still in use among

95

those sections of the population not completely under Pharisaic influence.

The temporary internal victory of the Sadducees probably brought a revival of the Early Hebrew script, especially, or shall we say exclusively, in conservative, non-Pharisaic and not-too-religious or orthodox circles. It is very difficult to know how far its use extended, because the only epigraphic remains of this period—or rather of a slightly later period, and of the following centuries, apart from the extant coins— are of a religious character, being either synagogal or funeral inscriptions, for which the Square Hebrew character was used (see Part III).

But, may we deduce from *Yadaim* iv. 5 that even at a later period there were still books and other documents written not only in Early Hebrew script, but on papyrus or leather? One may ask: are the *Leviticus* fragments and the other Early Hebrew Dead Sea fragments remains of such books?

The last Hasmonaeans themselves, by their intolerance, ambition and pride, had divided the nation, and so bitterly did the parties hate one another that party success was held more dear than national honor. At that time, and until the end of political independence, the civil and military power, so far as it was still in Jewish hands, belonged mainly to the Sadducees. On the other hand, the *Mishnah* records mainly the opinions of the Pharisaic party, and the standards to which Mishnaic rabbis aspired were certainly not those of the Sadducean party; the latter, it would seem, chiefly prevailed during the century before the destruction of Jerusalem.

It may be noted, indeed, that in the *Mishnah*, the powerful and ambitious Sadducees of the Hasmonaean monarchy figure only as an insignificant, discredited and heretical sect. For a certain period Judaism, at least Talmudic Judaism, came to be centered more and more in Babylonia, and began to represent a closer religious community; the sects—with the exception of the excommunicated Samaritans—ceased to exist and old quarrels on Palestinian soil passed away. The Early Hebrew script was forgotten and its history subsequently misunderstood.

PLATES

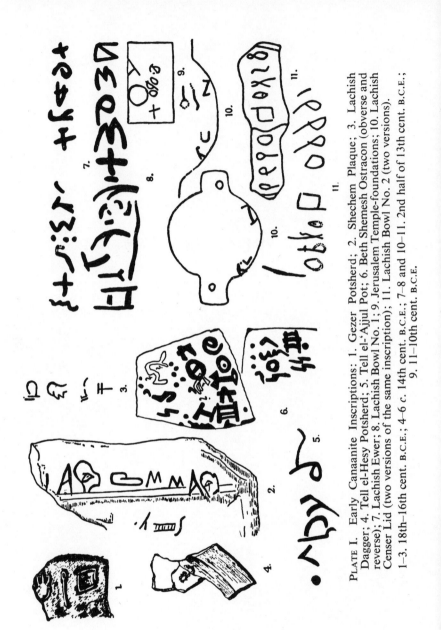

PLATE I. Early Canaanite Inscriptions: 1. Gezer Potsherd; 2. Shechem Plaque; 3. Lachish Dagger; 4. Tell el-Hesy Potsherd; 5. Tell el-'Ajjul Pot; 6. Beth Shemesh Ostracon (obverse and reverse); 7. Lachish Ewer; 8. Lachish Bowl No. 1; 9. Jerusalem Temple-foundations; 10. Lachish Censer Lid (two versions of the same inscription); 11. Lachish Bowl No. 2 (two versions). 1–3. 18th–16th cent. B.C.E.; 4–6 c. 14th cent. B.C.E.; 7–8 and 10–11. 2nd half of 13th cent. B.C.E.; 9. 11–10th cent. B.C.E.

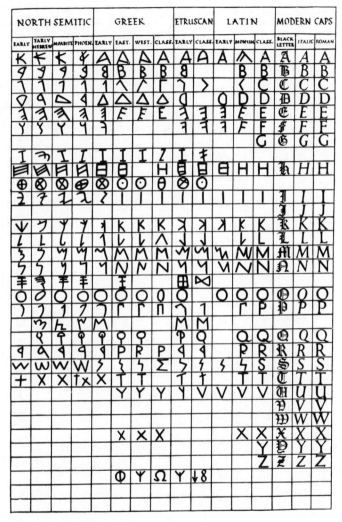

PLATE II. From North-Semitic (late 2nd Mill. B.C.E.) to modern capital letters.

	Gezer	Monumental	Cursive	Book-Hand	Coin-Script	Samaritan	Mod-Hebrew
1							א
2							ב
3							ג
4							ד
5							ה
6							ו
7							ז
8							ח
9							ט
10							י
11							כ
12							ל
13							מ
14							נ
15							ס
16							ע
17							פ
18							צ
19							ק
20							ר
21							ש
22							ת

A. Sylvester

PLATE III.   Early Hebrew alphabet: main styles.

19174

PLATE IV. Early Hebrew alphabet: Gezer Calendar (*c.* 1000 B.C.E.)

ci

North
(The Orig

South Semitic

Canaanite

Ethiopic

Greek   Phoenician   Early

Cyrillic   Etruscan

Russian and   Latin   Sam
Allied Alphabets

Modern West-
European Alphabets

PLATE V–VI.   Genealogy o

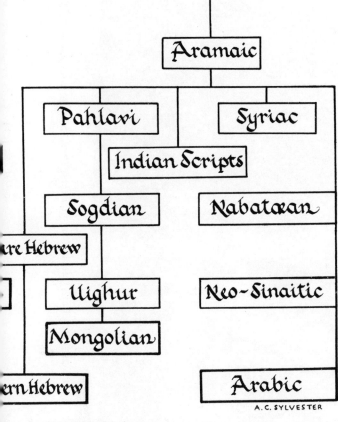

itic
lphabet)

Aramaic

Pahlavi   Syriac

Indian Scripts

Sogdian   Nabataean

re Hebrew

Uighur   Neo-Sinaitic

Mongolian

ern Hebrew   Arabic

A.C. SYLVESTER

w and other main alphabets.

PLATE VII. Early Hebrew monumental style: Siloam inscription (c. 700 B.C.E.)

PLATE VIII. Early Hebrew cursive style: Lachish Letter VI (early 6th cent. B.C.E.) (Courtesy of the Trustees of the late Sir Henry Wellcome.)

PLATE IX. Early Hebrew alphabet: selection of Maccabaean and Bar Kochba coins (135 B.C.E.–135 C.E.).

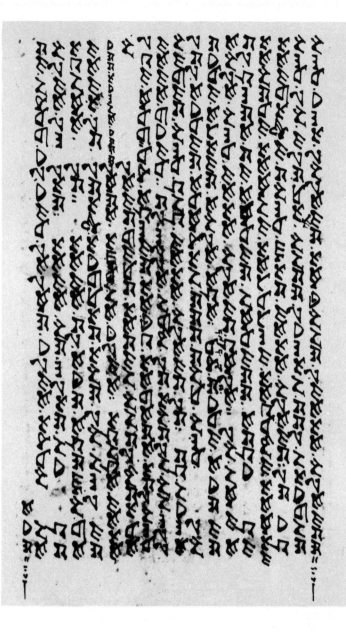

PLATE X.   Samaritan alphabet: Portion of a Pentateuch scroll (author's collection).

	Square Hebrew [Monumental]	Medieval Formal Styles	Rabbinic Styles	Cursive Styles	Contemporary	
					Cursive	Print
1						
2						
3						
4						
5						
6						
7						
8						
9						
10						
11						
12						
13						
14						
15						
16						
17						
18						
19						
20						
21						
22						

*Final Letters

A. Sylvester

PLATE XI. Square Hebrew alphabet: its development into modern Hebrew styles.

PLATE XII. Square Hebrew alphabet: Nash Papyrus
(*c*. 1st cent. B.C.E.) (Courtesy of the Cambridge
University Library.)

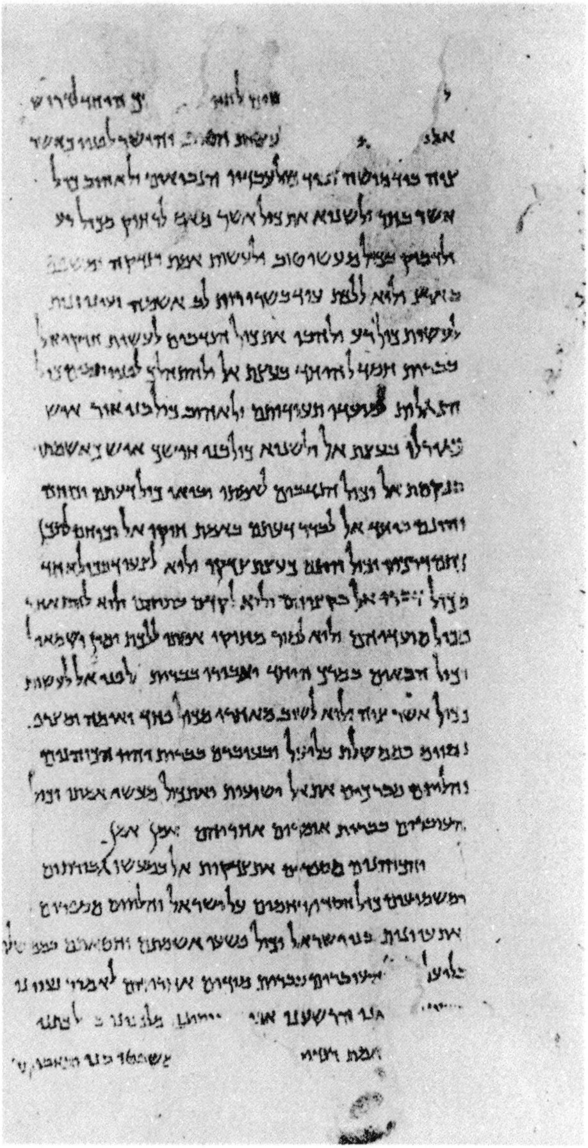

PLATE XIII. Square Hebrew alphabet: Dead Sea
Scrolls—Manual of Discipline, col. 1; ? 1st cent.
B.C.E. (Courtesy of the late Prof. E. L. Sukenik.)

PLATE XIV. Square Hebrew alphabet: Judaeo-Babylonian
vase with magic inscription; ? 8th cent. B.C.E.

PLATE XV. Square Hebrew monumental style: sepulchral inscription from Chufutkale (Crimea), dated to 443 (forgery?).

PLATE XVI. Hispano-Hebrew monumental style: sepulchral inscription dated to 15.5.1135, of Abishay bar Mar Ya'aqob, from Castrum Judaeorum (Puente del Castro), near Léon, Spain. (Courtesy of Prof. F. Cantera y Burgos, Madrid.)

וְשִׁפְּנִי טְמוּנֵי
חוֹל
וַיֵּלֶד
אָמַר בָּרוּךְ יד
מַרְחִיב גָּד י
כְּלָבִיא שָׁכֵן ·
וְטָרַף זְרוֹעַ אַף
קָדְקֹד וַיַּרְא ·
רֵאשִׁית לוֹ כִּי
שָׁם חֶלְקַת מְחֹקֵק
סָפוּן וַיֵּתֵא רָאשֵׁי
עָם צִדְקַת יְהֹוָה
עָשָׂה וּמִשְׁפָּטָיו
עִם יִשְׂרָאֵל

PLATE XVII. Formal Hebrew alphabet: Leningrad Pentateuch (Cod.
85), dated to 1132, from Jerusalem.

PLATE XVIII. Franco-German Hebrew formal and cursive styles of the 12th–13th cent. (Sassoon MS. No. 369, p. 201.) (Courtesy of Rabbi S. D. Sassoon.)

PLATE XIX–XX. Hispano-Hebrew monumental style: por

inscription in the Synagogue El Tránsito, at Toledo, Spain.

עריו בני ישראל | יהוה אל משה
לבשמ_חותם לביתא | בדרמם סבן בקהל
אמתם כמספר שמן | מדועד במאהאל לחרש
שב_לית מלזכר לגד | השד בשנה השבאד
לגלגלתם תבלה יה | לגאתם במאר_יז פיך
יושם מל כמ_שפאה ת | מיצרין לאמרי וביז
תבא ישראל לאחריה א | ובלליד יז עם משה
לבית אבחיהן בנן | במדברא רסלן בבן
מבקן שקמחן בי תם | ברמשם זבניא פהל
יברא לאי_גלואחהן | ליהואתערא בשתא
מבן עשרים | תבריאא ולבפמחזא מב
טפה_ומלחיה מ_יצא | מ_א קא ולגוגרים
צבא ביסר_אל תפקד | לבקמרי...
אתם לצבאתם אתה | ...ברדין ...
ואדרון _מבמ_עסדי | שאר _אדראשמ_לד

סב_ו ולע_לא מל את |
נפין חלא_מ_ש_ראל |
ק_מצן יד_ה_ה |
לחרלחיהן אח יצאחן |
ראתם_שמו בריד שרן |
ואתם יהו_איש אש |
איש לפ_שה אשראש |
ראש לבי_תא אבהיד_י ן |
הא_יושמפן יריחין |
גברא_גברא לשמ_אא |
פ_ר חש לבית אב_ד |
אחסמ_חידי הוא |
ואליה שמ_ית האקן |
האנשים_אשר קמ_ו |
יעביורו אהם_ם דריה |
ראתם_אל_צר_ צין כן |

PLATE XXI. Fourteenth-century (1344) German-Hebrew formal style (*De Castro Pentateuch*, Sassoon MS. No. 506, p. 411). (Courtesy of Rabbi S. D. Sassoon.)

cxviii

PLATE XXII. Hispano-Hebrew formal style of the 13th cent. (Cambridge University Library, MS. Add. 468, fol. 68 *recto*). (Courtesy of the C.U.L.)

PLATE XXIII. Late 15th-century (1476) Hispano-Hebrew formal style (MS. Kennicot 1, fol. 8 *verso*). (Courtesy of the Bodleian Library, Oxford.)

PLATE XXIV.   Early 15th-century (1415) Italo-Hebrew formal
and cursive styles (*Mahăzŏr*, Sassoon MS. No. 405, p. 486).
(Courtesy of Rabbi S. D. Sassoon.)

סדר חג הסוכות

בערב חג הסוכות דין מקדים על פניהם ואם הוי יום שני אין אומרים
יענה ובמנחה מתפללין כשאר הימים וכערבית אם הוי חול
מתפלל כמו בחול ואם הוי שבת כמו שבת ואומר ופרוש עלינו
סוכת שלומך יום הוא שבת ויזמר וישמרו

אלה מועדי יֵי מקראי קדש אשר תקראו אותם במועדם

ואומר קדוש על לעולו
ומתפללים מזון ומזחיה והגול הקדוש

אתה בחרתנו מכל העמים אהבת
אותנו ורצית בנו
ורוממתנו מכל
הלשונות קדשתנו
במיצותיך וקרבתנו מלכנו לעבורתך ושמך הגדול והקדוש ע
עלינו קראת ותתן לנו יֵי אלהינו באהבה שבתות למנוחה ו
מועדים לשמחה וחגים וזמנים לששון את יום השבת הזה ו
את יום חג הסוכות הזה זמן שמחתינו מקרא קדש זכר ליציאת
מיצרים

אלהינו ואלהי אבותינו יעלה ויבא יגיע ויראה וירצה
וישמע ויפקר ויזכר זכרוננו ופקרוננו וזכרון אבותינו
זכרון ירושלים עיִרך וזכרון משיח בן דוד עבדך
וזכרון כל עמך בית ישראל לפניך לטובה לחן ולחסד ולרחמים

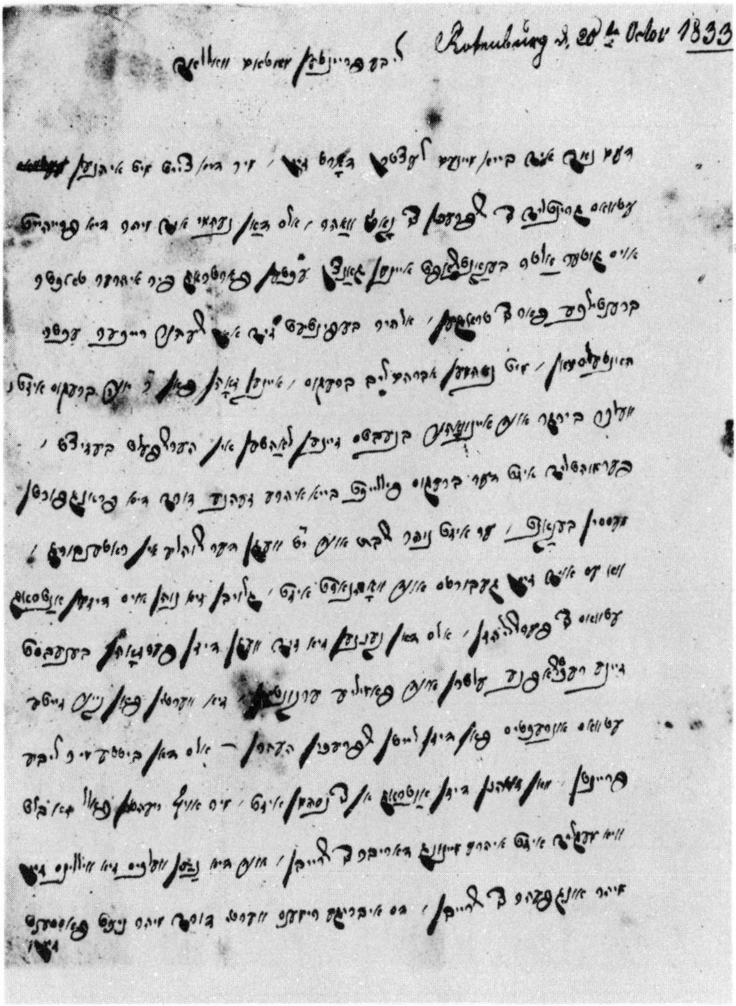

PLATE XXVI. Modern Hebrew alphabet, cursive style: its
adaptation to Yiddish (Private letter—Courtesy of Dr.
O. Simon).

PLATE XXVII. Modern Hebrew alphabet in styles of print, literary hand and cursive.

PART III

SQUARE HEBREW ALPHABET
Pl. XI–XXVII

CHAPTER 1

ITS ORIGIN—OLDEST INSCRIPTIONS

THE MAIN LITERARY source for the origin of the Square Hebrew alphabet, the ancestor of the modern Hebrew script, is this passage, *Sanhedrin* 21b:

> "Mar Zutra or, as some say, Mar 'Uqbā said: Originally the Torah was given to Israel in Hebrew characters and in the sacred tongue; it was given again to them, in the days of Ezra, in the *ketabh 'ashshurî* ('Assyrian writing') and in the Aramaic tongue; they chose for Israel the 'Assyrian' script and the sacred tongue, and left to the *hedyoṭoth* the Hebrew characters and the Aramaic tongue. Who are meant by the *hedyoṭoth*? R. Ḥisda (a teacher of the school of Sura, *d.* 309) said: The Kutheans (that is, apparently, the Samaritans). What is meant by the Hebrew script? R. Ḥisda said: The *libbona'ah* script."

CHANGE OF CHARACTER ACCORDING TO TRADITION

In other words, according to this talmudical passage, in the period of Ezra, that is, in the fifth–fourth century B.C.E., the *Torah* was re-written in the Aramaic script which had been introduced from Assyria(?) and Israel subsequently continued to use this script for the *Torah*, while the *hedyoṭoth* continued to use the Hebrew writing: see also p. 92 ff.

The end of *Sanhedrin* 21b and the beginning of 22a are far from clear. There we read:

> ". . . concerning Ezra, it is stated: For Ezra had prepared his heart to expound the Law of the Lord (his God) to do it and to teach Israel statutes and judgments (*Ezra* vii. 10). And even though the Torah was not given through him, its writing was changed through him, as it is written: And the writing of the letter was written in the Aramaic script and translated into Aramaic (*Ezra* iv. 7). And again

it is written: And they could not read the writing nor make known to the King the interpretation thereof (*Dan.* v. 8). Further it is written: And he shall write a copy (*mishneh*) of this Torah (*Deut.* xvii. 18) in writing which was destined to be changed. Why is it called Assyrian? Because it came from Assyria. It has been taught: Rabbi said, The Torah was originally given to Israel in this (Assyrian) writing. When they sinned, it was changed into 'splinter-like' (variant: 'pricking') script. But when they repented, they (the Assyrian characters) were re-introduced. . . . Why was it named 'Assyrian' (*'ashshurîth*)? Because its script was upright (*me'ushshar*). R. Simeon b. Eliezer said on the authority of R. Eliezer b. Parta, who spoke on the authority of R. Eliezer of Modin: This writing (of the Law) was never changed, for it is written: the hooks (*waws*) of the pillars (*Exod.* xxvii. 10); as the word 'pillars' had not changed, neither had the word *wawim*. Again it is written: And unto the Jews, according to their writing and language (*Esth.* viii. 9): as their language had not changed, neither had their writing. Then, how shall I interpret the words 'And he shall write for himself a copy (*mishneh*) of this Law'? As indicating the need of two written Torahs: the one to go in and out with him; the other to be deposited by him in his treasure-house. The one that is to go in and out with him, he is to write in the form of phylacteries and attach to his arm. . . ."

This passage partly contradicts the previous one: the change of characters is no longer attributed to "the days of Ezra", but is assigned to Ezra himself. Moreover, here we find a tradition of a double change, the second change being a return to the original characters, unless there was also a tradition that the *Torah* was originally written in a script which was more like the Aramaic alphabet than the post-exilic Early Hebrew–Samaritan script.

However, if Ezra had adapted the Aramaic script to, or adopted it for, the Hebrew tongue, the author of the *Book of Ezra* would certainly have found an opportunity of mentioning so important an event, especially as he emphasizes that Ezra "was a ready scribe in the Law of Moses, which the Lord God of Israel had given" (*Ezra* vii. 6), and relates how "in the days of Artaxerxes wrote Bishlam, Mithredath, Tabeel and the rest of their companions, unto Artaxerxes king of Persia; and the writing of the letter was written in the Aramaic character and translated (from Hebrew?) into the Aramaic tongue" (*Ezra* iv. 7). On the whole, it would seem, there was a constant Jewish tradition—it is supported by the passages *Megill. Jer.* i. 71*b* and *Sota Jer.* vii. 21*c*, and also by the writings of the Fathers of the Church—that in the period of Ezra a new script, which originated in Assyria (*sc.* Mesopotamia (?)) or Syria or otherwise came from Assyria (Mesopotamia), began to be used for the writing of the *Torah*. It was adopted by Israel, or should we say by the religious leaders of Israel, probably those who had returned from exile in Babylon.

POLITICAL AND RELIGIOUS BACKGROUND

It is well known that hardly any information about the life of the Palestinian Jews from Nebuchadnezzar's conquest in 586 B.C.E. to the events preceding the Maccabaean rebellion in 168–7 B.C.E. has survived, except what may be gleaned from the Books of Haggai, Zechariah, Nehemiah, and possibly Ezra. From Haggai and Zechariah we learn that the Temple was rebuilt in 520–516 B.C.E., and also that some Jews, "stirred by the widespread insurrections raging when Darius (521–485) ascended the Persian throne, believed that the Lord was shaking the kingdoms in order to give to the Jews independence and dominion".

Thus, Zerubbabel, a descendant of David, was crowned as the Messianic king, but he was "liquidated" at once, though the Persian authorities granted the Jews complete freedom in religious and cultural matters. The liberal policy of the Persians is particularly evident in the activity of Nehemiah about the middle of the fifth century B.C.E., who reorganized the spiritual and social life of the pitiful congregation in Jerusalem and restored the city's fortifications.

In Prof. R. H. Pfeiffer's opinion, this liberal policy was ideally suited to further the transition from kingdom to nation, from state to holy congregation. In this connection, the restoration of the *Torah* proved far more significant for the whole course of Jewish history than the rebuilding of the Temple. In the course of time, the study of the *Torah* brought into being the Synagogue, which became the most vital and original institution of Judaism.

Jewish tradition extols Ezra as the restorer of the *Torah*. Ezra, about the mid-fifth century B.C.E., marks the opening of a new period, a new stage of development. In Talmudic tradition Ezra's work is second in importance only to that of Moses. If Moses was the real founder of the Jewish religion, Ezra stood forth at a most critical period to save the Jewish religion, and with it the national life, from relapsing into decay through contact with Gentile ideas and practices.

A leading non-Jewish student of the Pharisees, the late R. Travers Herford, has pointed out how great the national danger was in Ezra's time. The small, weak community in and around Jerusalem was like sheep in the midst of wolves, exposed to the attractions of apostasy through want of any strong convictions, any definite principle in whose defence they might be rallied. The national vitality was apparently ebbing away, and what Ezra did was, basically, to stop that fatal process and provide for the spiritual energy of his people an object worthy to live for and, if need be, to die for. The *Torah* was proclaimed as the guide of life for the Jew; Ezra was the first of the *Sopherim* or "Scribes", who made it their business to "interpret" the *Torah*. But it took many centuries before their work achieved any practical results.

SOPHERIM

The period after Ezra is likewise shrouded in obscurity, and only a few dim rays penetrate here and there. On the whole, Judaea remained destitute. Under Alexander the Great, the Ptolemies, and the early Seleucids, the Jews were apparently granted considerable autonomy and were allowed to develop their culture undisturbed as long as they paid the taxes and remained submissive, but they began to be conscious of those powerful and varied conditions which are summed up under the name of Hellenism. These influences made the simple and peaceful practice of strictly Jewish religious life at least very difficult.

From the time of Ezra, down to about 270 B.C.E., the "interpreting" and teaching of the *Torah* was apparently carried out by the *Sopherim*, who were organized in the *Keneseth Hagedolah* (the "Great Assembly") which, according to Jewish tradition, was founded by Ezra, though very little is known of its history or activity, or indeed of this period

generally. However, ancient tradition ascribes to the *Sopherim*
certain acts, decisions, and declarations which, in Travers
Herford's opinion, can only be understood as proceeding from
a body of teachers and not from an individual. Simeon the
Just, first half of the third century B.C.E., appears to have been
the last *Sopher*. Then, for nearly a century, the religious history
of the Jews is a blank, except for the information of the
Tractate *Aboth* (i. 3–4) that Antigonos of Socho, whose Greek
name is a noteworthy indication of Hellenistic influence, was a
disciple of Simeon the Just, and that Jose b. Joezer and Jose b.
Jochanan received the *Torah* from these notable teachers.

SANHEDRIN

About 200 B.C.E. a new organization was founded, known
as the *Sanhedrin* (term derived from the Greek word for
"council", *sunédrion*) or Senate, the chief council of the
Community for all public affairs, thus also the supreme
authority in religious matters. It was a composite body of
priests and laymen—indeed, the first central authority with
laymen as members—presided over by the High Priest. Some
of the members, and particularly the priests, favored a policy
of compromise with Hellenistic thought, whilst others, who
included teachers amongst their number, opposed it out of
loyalty to the *Torah*.

PHARISEES AND TANNAÏM

In the joy and pride of the Hasmonaean victory, principles
were forgotten and no one would wish to associate himself
with those who had openly preached "ignoble" submission.
But the differences between the opposing parties were deep-
seated, and somewhat before 105 B.C.E. the breach between
the Pharisees and the Sadducees occurred: see p. 95 f.

It was a trial of strength between the purely religious and
the political theory of Jewish national life. Indeed, it must
be borne in mind that the Pharisees were a non-political party
whose chief concern was for religion, but they were not hostile
to the idea of an independent state; and the Sadducees while
by no means indifferent to religion, combined with it the
conduct of political affairs. However, when with the final
Roman victory the political catastrophe was complete, the
religious vitality of the nation was still unimpaired, and as a

131

result, the victory of the Pharisees over the Sadducees was overwhelming.

Hillel, who was born in Babylonia, was for about forty years one of the acknowledged leaders of the Judaean community. He exemplified the Pharisaic standpoint at its best, and was the creator of a school of *Tannaïm*. The youngest and most famous disciple of Hillel was Jochanan ben Zakkai, the founder of the Academy in Jabneh; this became the center of Jewish life and thought, and was instrumental in saving the *Torah* from probable annihilation in the national disaster of the year 70 C.E.; it thus assured the survival of Judaism.

SQUARE HEBREW SCRIPT VERSUS EARLY HEBREW SCRIPT

It is pertinent to understand why the Aramaic script was then adopted for writing the *Torah*. At that time Aramaic was the *lingua franca*: see also p. 42. Indeed, we may assume that the Aramaic script was the only script used in the Jewish schools of Babylonia, at least in the second or third generation of the Exile.

It will suffice to refer to the passage in *Tosefta, Megillah* ii. 5, in which we read that Rabbi Meir (see p. 173), who was a scribe by profession, could find no *megillah* written in *'ibhrît* in the parts of Asia he visited, so that he had to write one from memory.

It may be assumed that even in Palestine few scrolls in *'ibhrît* were available.

The questions how and when Square Hebrew originated are not difficult to answer and are dealt with in other parts of this book. More significant are the questions: Why was it deemed necessary to replace the beautiful Early Hebrew literary-hand, the ancient script of the Hebrew kings and prophets—in short, *the Hebrew* script? Why was the Aramaic script adopted when, in that period, it was certainly not as beautiful as the Early Hebrew? Why was this Hebrew–Aramaic script, which we know as the Square Hebrew, proclaimed as holy—this being the meaning of the Talmudic term "renders the hands unclean"? There is only one answer to these questions: To preserve the essence of Judaism, the *Torah*, and the unity of the Jewish people.

This answer, considered against the historical, political, and religious background as summarized above, will explain many obscure points.

For at least five hundred years, two scripts were in current use in Palestine, in addition to Greek which in the Hellenistic period was well known in the aristocratic circles of Jerusalem: (*a*) the old national script or Early Hebrew; and (*b*) the script of the *lingua franca* of the whole Near East, Aramaic. But outside Palestine, and particularly in Mesopotamia, soon after the disappearance of the first generation of the Exile, the Early Hebrew script fell into disuse and was forgotten.

Deprived of their leadership, i.e., the dominant nobility of Jerusalem, the leading craftsmen and traders—the masses of Judaean peasantry who were left on their farms and in their vineyards, persisted with their popular religion, their language and script, and their patriotism, but they were unable to produce a spiritual successor to the Jerusalem Temple, such as the Jabneh Academy was after the destruction of Jerusalem in the year 70 C.E., or, indeed, any cultural center.

In Babylon, by degrees the Jews learned to make the best of their life. They were at liberty to hold real estate, to carry on business and to prosper; several were in a position to gain considerable wealth. According to the old–new principle *ubi bene ibi patria* many may soon have forgotten the old home and become apostates. It is superfluous to point to modern conditions.

A genius such as Ezra was aware of the dangers involved, and he had of course a great following. It seems that the spiritual leaders who lived in Babylonia did not credit the home community with enough force to bring about a renaissance on their own initiative. On the other hand the actual course of events proves that careful plans had been laid at long range in Babylon for the reorganization of Jewish life after the return to the motherland.

This became possible by gaining personal favor with the King of Kings of the Persian Empire through influential Jews residing at his court: "and the King granted him all his request according to the hand of the Lord his God upon him". "This Ezra went up from Babylon; and he was a ready scribe in the Law of Moses" (*Ezra* vii. 6). The edict of the Persian king Artaxerxes permitted Ezra to bring back a further contingent of Jewish leaders from Babylon, and to overhaul the state of affairs in Judaea (*Ezra* vii. 12–26).

133

It is difficult to say whether the script employed by Ezra and the *Sopherim* (see p. 130 f.) was the Aramaic or the Early Hebrew. If it was the former, which is highly probable, there was no question of prohibiting the use of the latter, which was in very limited use for several more centuries. At the same time, apparently there was no great opposition on the part of the local population to the introduction of the new script.

A few facts may be mentioned at this point: (1) the Aramaic script had already been in use for several centuries; (2) the level of culture, education, and literacy, appears to have been deplorable, as aptly described, for instance, by A. Spiro in "Samaritans, Tobiads, and Judahites in Pseudo-Philo", *Proceedings of The American Academy for Jewish Research*, XX, 1951, pp. 279 ff., *passim*; (3) the local population of Palestine which used the Early Hebrew script lacked leaders of the stamp of Ezra who could effectively oppose the new reforms.

Still, the Early Hebrew script was an object of such local attachment that for several centuries it was used side by side with the new script. Jews have always preferred to use varied scripts. But the Pharisees realized that they had to concentrate on one script. Hence—I would suggest—both scripts were permitted, but one became "holy", although it took our sages centuries to come to this decision.

ORIGIN OF THE SQUARE HEBREW SCRIPT

There can be little doubt that the Square Hebrew alphabet derived from the Aramaic script. It is generally believed, in accordance with the Jewish tradition previously referred to, that the Early Hebrew alphabet was completely superseded by the Aramaic alphabet during the Babylonian exile, and that the Aramaic alphabet therefore became the only parent of the Square Hebrew, and hence of the modern Hebrew alphabet.

This opinion, though on the whole correct, should be accepted with some reservation. The *ketabh merubā*, or "Square Script", or *ketabh ashshurî*, or "Assyrian Script", although based mainly on the Aramaic alphabet, was—it would seem— strongly influenced by the Early Hebrew alphabet.

A tomb inscription from 'Araq el-Emir in Transjordan, can be regarded as written in a transitional script between the Aramaic and the Early Hebrew character on the one hand,

and the Square Hebrew on the other. This inscription, which will be discussed below, has been variously attributed to 176 B.C.E., to the third century B.C.E., to about 400 B.C.E., and to the late sixth or early fifth century B.C.E.

STANDARDIZATION OF SQUARE HEBREW

At any rate, a distinctive Palestinian Jewish type of script—which we can definitely regard as the Square Hebrew script—can be traced from the second and the first centuries B.C.E. According to Prof. W. F. Albright, it became standardized just before the Christian era. It is from this script that the modern Hebrew alphabet, in all its styles, eventually developed.

This development, as one may surmise, was gradual and purely external, that is in the shapes of the single letters. From the internal standpoint, that is considering phonetic values of the letters, there has been no development, though it has to be borne in mind that for several letters (such as *waw, heth, teth, 'ayin, sade, qoph, shin—sin, beth—bheth, kaph—khaph, pe—phe, taw—thaw*) the exact original phonetic value is still uncertain.

When the Square Hebrew character became standardized, it took the form which, with insignificant changes, we have now. The minute rules laid down by the Talmud as to calligraphy and consonantal orthography made further development of the Square Hebrew impossible. Therefore, the writing of the MSS. scarcely varies through the centuries, except in style: for instance, the German and Polish Jews preferred the somewhat angular script, known as *Tam*, whereas the Spanish Jews preferred the more rounded script, known as *Welsh*.

STANDARD SCRIPT FOR STANDARD TEXT

Indeed, the veneration shown for the Sacred Scriptures in the period of standardization of the script naturally led to a greater care in copying them. Moreover, as soon as the Scriptures obtained canonical authority they were used in divine service and became the standard of doctrine in life: the necessity of having one *standard text* naturally asserted itself.

Faithful and corrected copies, especially of such books as were publicly read, existed at an earlier period. But after the

135

destruction of Jerusalem, when Judaism was governed by the authority of the Rabbis, a uniform standard text was certainly employed. Josephus, in *Contra Apion*. I. viii, and even Philo, as we know from Eusebius, *Praeparatio evangelica*, VIII. vi. 7, speak of the great care bestowed by the Jews upon their Sacred writings.

Moreover, the Talmud bears witness that the consonantal determination of the text of the Scriptures was practically finished long before the Talmudic era was closed (see also p. 153). The post-Talmudic treatises *Massekheth Sopherim* and *Massekheth Sepher Torah* contain full details for copying Sacred texts. Further, the way in which the Massoretes presented the individuality of the several Biblical books and periods is remarkable, and proves that intentional or arbitrary changes of the text or of orthography were not allowed. Interesting too is the reference to three kinds of *qerê*, "reading" (corrections suggested by the critics in the margin but not inserted in the text, which contain the *ketîbh*, what is "written"): thus, the margins contain the annotations: "(to be) read but not written" or "written but not read" or else "read (one way) but written (another)". But no correction of the text itself was allowed!

FINAL LETTERS

The development of the Square Hebrew style, as already said, does not present great changes; the changes in detail, whatever their importance for the palaeographer, have no great significance for the general reader. Thus, the standardized script of the *Torah* scrolls—the constancy being due mainly to the Talmudic scrupulous and detailed prescriptions—is in fact in all its essentials the same script which was used nearly two thousand years ago.

In the Square Hebrew style, unlike the Early Hebrew, while there are resemblances, at least superficially, between some letters, which cause ambiguity in reading (*beth* and initial *kaph*; *gimel* and initial *nun*; *waw* and *zayin*, *he* and *ḥeth*, and partly also *taw*; in some early documents also *waw* and *yodh*), there are five letters which have dual forms, one when initial or medial, the other when final (see also p. 177); these letters are *kaph*, *mem*, *nun*, *pe* and *ṣade*.

The dual forms in great part go back to the period before

136

the various offshoots of the Aramaic script assumed their distinctive features; they are found, indeed, in some third-century B.C.E. cursive documents in Egypt, in Nabataean inscriptions, and in the earliest Square Hebrew inscriptions and other documents. In some early documents, the letters *'aleph*, *he* and *taw* also have dual forms.

The problem of the origin of duality in form is outside the scope of the present work. We may assume that this origin *mutatis mutandis* was analogous to the development of the letters I–J and U–V in the Western alphabets, dual forms being used contemporaneously for a certain period with the same phonetic value. Basing himself on Talmudic sources and available manuscripts and inscriptions, Prof. Tur-Sinai has suggested that in earlier times both dual forms had been used either as final letters or as non-finals.

Gradually, however, the tendency developed to use the *mem* with the ligature, or connecting stroke to the left, as the non-final, on the analogy of the letters *kaph*, *nun*, *pe* and *ṣade*, which had developed from the original final forms. It was during the second century C.E.—according to Prof. Tur-Sinai—that our present Square Hebrew script, in its current form, became more or less fixed, and it was only in this period that the consistent Massoretic tradition regarding the use of the dual forms of the letters *kaph*, *mem*, *nun*, *pe*, *ṣade* was established.

OLDEST INSCRIPTIONS

Before the discovery of the celebrated Dead Sea Scrolls, several Square Hebrew inscriptions were known belonging mainly to the first century B.C.E. and the succeeding centuries: they were found in Palestine, Syria, North Africa, and Italy on rocks, tombs or ossuaries, in synagogues and catacombs. Not all these inscriptions are in monumental or lapidary style, as are for instance the tomb inscription of the Bene Ḥezir or the slab inscription of Uzziah; the graffiti scratched on ossuaries are in a semi-cursive style; and the dipinti, or painted inscriptions are in a cursive style.

TOBIAS INSCRIPTION

The earliest inscription, that of Tobias, has already been mentioned. It is very short, containing five letters only, *ṭ w b y h* (i.e. the name Tobiah), but it is repeated twice; it is deeply incised in rock at the entrance to a cave in the ruin of Qaṣr el-'Abd at 'Araq el-Emir. This inscription, as has been said, variously assigned to dates between the late sixth century and 176 B.C.E., is perhaps in a transitional Early Hebrew—Square Hebrew style: see also p. 134 f.

GEZER BOUNDARY INSCRIPTIONS

Of more recent but also of more certain date is the *t ḥ m g z r*, "(Sabbath) Boundary (of) Gezer" inscription, discovered in five examples cut in the rocks of the ancient city of Gezer. It is generally agreed that this inscription may be assigned to the first third of the first century B.C.E., and certainly to not later than 63 B.C.E., in which year, with the conquest of Judaea by Pompey, the city passed into Roman occupation and was soon deserted. The Gezer Boundary-inscription may be regarded as the earliest document written in a pure lapidary Square Hebrew style.

FRAGMENTARY COIN-INSCRIPTIONS

The earliest extant dated Square Hebrew inscriptions are fourteen fragmentary coin-inscriptions, some having been recently discovered, and others having been brought to our notice following this discovery. They have been published by A. Kindler, in *The Jaffa Hoard of Alexander Jannaeus* ("Israel Expl. Journ.", IV–1954, pp. 170–85; and "Publication of the Israel Numism. Soc.", I 1954, pp. 170–85), and *On the Discovery of the Coins of Alexander Yannai* ("Bull. of the Israel Explor. Soc." XX–1956, pp. 51–53; in Hebrew). These coins are dated to 90–85 B.C.E.

It is interesting to note that these coins—the only ones which bear Square Hebrew inscriptions—were issued by Alexander Jannaeus (103–76 B.C.E.), the first Maccabaean ruler who not only styled himself king on his coins, but also stamped his name and title in Greek (see p. 91).

OSSUARY INSCRIPTIONS

In Prof. Albright's opinion, roughly contemporary with the Gezer Boundary-inscription, is the Bethphage ossuary lid-inscription, preserved in the Louvre Museum. This graffito, containing a list of laborers, consists of twenty-seven lines, written in a cursive or semi-cursive style; it is thus the earliest preserved inscription in such a style. Prof. Albright points out that the eight cases of *he* are written in the archaic style; two of *taw* written with the loop as generally in the *Nash Papyrus* (see p. 142 f.). "Otherwise the characters are typically Herodian, and there are apparently no ligatures nor medial characters extending below the base-line."

A certain number of Square Hebrew inscriptions in lapidary style, as well as graffiti scratched on ossuaries in semi-cursive style, and dipinti in cursive style, are attributed by S. Klein and other scholars to the last century of the Second Temple (about 30 B.C.E.–70 C.E.).

S. Klein's collection of the inscriptional material (*Jüdisch-palästinisches Corpus Inscriptionum*, R. Löwit, Vienna and Berlin, 1920) contains 103 ossuary and sepulchral Hebrew inscriptions and 14 Hebrew synagogal inscriptions, the former being mostly from the district of Jerusalem, the latter mainly from Galilee and Transjordan. Unfortunately, the book does not contain photographs or facsimiles of the inscriptions, hence its use for the present purpose is rather limited. Several Hebrew synagogue-inscriptions were published by the late Prof. E. L. Sukenik in *Ancient Synagogues in Palestine and Greece*, Oxford University Press, 1934; *The Ancient Synagogue of el-Hammeh*, Rubin Mass, Jerusalem, 1935, and in other important publications, all containing excellent photographs and facsimiles.

One of the longest is the sepulchral inscription of the Bene-Ḥezir in the so-called Tomb of St. James, in the Kidron Valley. In De Vogüé's opinion, accepted by leading scholars, the tomb of the Bene-Ḥezir belonged to the priestly family from which came three High-priests during the reigns of Herod and Archelaus; thus, the inscription would belong probably to the end of Herod's reign (4 B.C.E.) or a few years later.

UZZIAH SLAB

Slightly later is the Uzziah Slab: it is an Aramaic lapidary inscription, which mentions the removal of the bones of King Uzziah. Prof. Albright and other scholars assign it to a late period of Jewish autonomy, either that of Herod the Great (37–4 B.C.E.) or that of Agrippa (37–44 C.E.).

QUEEN HELENA INSCRIPTION

The only inscription which can be dated with reasonable accuracy is the sarcophagus-epigraph of Queen Ṣarah-Helena of Adiabene, found in the "Tomb of the Kings", at Jerusalem. Although not all scholars agree that Queen Ṣrh—as the name is given in the Hebrew portion of the Syriac-Hebrew inscription—is Queen Helena of Adiabene, this identification is certain, and the inscription is to be dated to 50–60 C.E.

OTHER OSSUARY INSCRIPTIONS

Amongst the earliest of the semi-cursive graffiti on ossuaries are two groups assigned by Albright to the late first century B.C.E. and the very beginning of the Christian era. One group is in the tomb of the family of Shim'on Sava. In this group Albright notices the archaic form of the letter *he* in writing the name *Y h w s f* = Joseph, the looped *taw* used in *sh t* and *'sh t*. The second group, which is closely related to the first in script and personal names, discovered twenty years ago by Prof. E. L. Sukenik near the village Siloam (see pp. 58 and 69 f.), contained twelve ossuaries, but some bear no inscription and others are inscribed in Greek. Those inscribed in Hebrew contain Hebrew personal names, several names being rather unusual. One ossuary contains the name Shim'on bar Yannai (or Jannaeus) and the name Sheth (or Seth), probably two members of the same family. The unusual name Sheth is, however, known from another group of ossuaries (Eleazar ben Sheth). Other names are the Biblical Yehoshua' and Yehonathan, an uncertain name *H g r m n*, and two interesting feminine names, Salome and Martha *barath* Ḥananiah.

To a later period belongs the group of the Kallon ossuaries, found near Katamon, south-west of Jerusalem; one of the Kallons, Yo'azar ben Kallon, married Shelamṣiyon, daughter of Gamala, the latter being identified with the High-priest Gamala (after 63 C.E.). The family Kallon belonged to the highest nobility of Jerusalem, was related by marriage to King Herod, and regarded itself as descending from Jeshebeab, mentioned in 1 *Chr.* xxiv. 13. Other ossuary-graffiti are slightly later, as they do not contain any archaic forms.

Prof. Albright has rightly pointed out that the cursive dipinti and the semi-cursive graffiti, apart from the obvious differences in style also differ in the use of ligatures. Curiously enough, while in other scripts ligatures are less frequent in lapidary than in cursive documents, in the present case they are extremely rare in such inscriptions except in the words *bar*, "son", and *benei*, "sons of". Indeed, in Albright's opinion,

140

cursive Square Hebrew increasingly avoided ligatures after the first half of the first century B.C.E.

DEAD SEA COPPER SCROLLS

Of unique significance are the Qumran copper-scrolls—two rolled strips of copper discovered on March 20, 1952, in Qumran Cave 3 (see p. 146 f.)—all the remaining Dead Sea documents being on leather, papyrus, and—in a few rare instances—pottery. The decipherment of the scrolls was far from easy. No metallic copper remained in the copper-strips, and the rolls had to be cut in bands, before any reading could be attempted. In August 1955 and January 1956 the scrolls were brought to Manchester, where they were "operated" on by Prof. H. Wright Baker of the Manchester College of Technology. No part of the text was lost in the process.

Originally, the rolls formed a single document, about 96 inches by 12 inches, composed of three "sheets" or strips riveted together. Each "sheet" contained four columns of text, of between 13 and 17 lines to the column. In Abbé J. T. Milik's opinion, the script is of the middle of the first century C.E. One would assume that an inscription on copper would be in monumental style. Indeed, in Milik's opinion, apparently the scribe attempted to engrave his work in an elegant formal script, but he was unsuccessful. He occasionally uses the forms and ligatures of the current style along with monumental letters, and often confuses graphically several letters of the monumental style. Abbé Milik has also noticed frequent slips and errors in orthography and grammatical and lexical peculiarities.

CHAPTER 2

OLDEST LITERARY DOCUMENTS

Pl. XII–XIII

THE EARLIEST EXTANT datable Hebrew Biblical manuscripts belong to the ninth and tenth centuries C.E. These will be dealt with in Chapter 4. Some hundred thousand fragments of Hebrew Biblical manuscripts were discovered in the famous Cairo *Genizah*—the lumber room in which defective manuscripts were laid aside—and these partly belong to the seventh or eighth century C.E.

There are not many Hebrew papyri extant, and they are mainly of late date. Some are in the British Museum, some in the Bodleian Library at Oxford. An extremely interesting Hebrew papyrus codex (now dismantled) has been preserved at the Cambridge University Library. Some Hebrew fragments preserved in the Bodleian Library, partly unpublished, are assigned to the third–fifth centuries C.E. Another Bodleian papyrus has been variously attributed to the sixth or the eighth century C.E.

DURA EUROPOS PARCHMENT

Prior to the discovery of the Dead Sea Scrolls, the earliest extant Hebrew parchment roll-fragment was that discovered in 1932–3 at Dura Europos on the Middle Euphrates; it contains a prayer, which was probably part of the synagogue service. It may have belonged to the latest synagogue of Dura, which was built about 245 C.E. or even to the earlier synagogue, and, thus, may be assigned to the late second or the early third century C.E.

NASH PAPYRUS

Pl. XII

The Nash Papyrus, preserved in the University Library of Cambridge, belongs to a much earlier period. It contains the Hebrew Decalogue and the *Shema'*; previously assigned to the first or second century C.E., it has now been assigned by Albright to the second or first century B.C.E. The importance of this document very much increased after the discovery of the Dead Sea Scrolls, because of the similar style of writing.

CRITERIA FOR DATING WRITTEN DOCUMENTS

Before we come to the vexed problem of the Dead Sea Scrolls, it may be as well to point out the great difficulties involved in the dating of these celebrated manuscripts. Strictly speaking, as already emphasized, any scholar dating a written document should, for comparison, take documents written in the same region, in the same style, and on the same material. As no such documents are available, it is unwise at present to be dogmatic regarding the date of these scrolls, or indeed, as to their importance for Biblical study, and philological, theological, or allied research, as well as for identifying the sect of the writers of the scrolls.

In the absence of dated Square Hebrew manuscripts written on leather in Palestine, other documents may be considered for comparison. It goes without saying that certain stylistic features in a given script are due to the natural evolution of the script, and can be found on different media in the same region, whilst other features are typical of the evolution of writing on the same writing material, and with the same tools, though produced in another region. Material of both types can be found for comparison with the writing on the Dead Sea Scrolls. On the one hand, we have inscriptions on stone in the Palmyrene and the Nabataean scripts, both being developments of Aramaic scripts, and on the other, Aramaic papyri written in the Jewish colonies in Egypt. Finally, other features or peculiarities should be borne in mind, such as those due to the individuality of the writer or to his lack of skill.

The reader who appreciates all these points of difficulty and the fact that in certain scripts, such as the Hebrew, a *ductus* or style was not always limited to a certain school of scribes or to a certain limited area or to a certain limited period, will easily understand why the dating of the Dead Sea Scrolls is still debatable. It has to be added that in the present work we are only dealing with the problem of writing.

THE DEAD SEA SCROLLS
Pl. XIII

The focus of world interest during the last years of the 'forties and the first years of the present decade, has been the sensational discovery of Hebrew Biblical and non-Biblical scrolls by a goat-herd in a cave near the Dead Sea. Although the main storm has calmed, at least in the daily press and the popular magazines, discussion of the date of the Scrolls, and their philological, Biblical, and theological significance, continues unabated. There is now an extensive literature on the various problems.

FIRST DISCOVERIES

The epoch-making discovery was made in the late spring-months of 1947, but a considerable time elapsed before the documents came into the hands of anyone capable of appreciating their importance. Indeed, so astonishing was the discovery that there was at first a great deal of scepticism about the authenticity of the new finds. Leading Catholic, Protestant, and Jewish scholars considered the newly found manuscripts forgeries or medieval.

The first discovery was made by a Bedouin goat-herd of the Ta'amireh tribe, named Muhammad adh-Dhib ("The Wolf"), in a natural cave, now known as Qumran Cave 1, high up the steep rock in the Wady Qumran, some seven miles south of Jericho along the track to 'Ain Feshkha, over one mile to the west of the shores of the Dead Sea, and about 1000 yards north of Khirbet Qumran, which is a small ancient site. Apparently in the first instance only three scrolls were taken away; these are now known as *Isaiah Scroll A, Manual of Discipline,* and *Habakkuk Commentary.* In the subsequent clandestine excavation at least eight more manuscripts came to light. Thus, all told, eleven manuscripts on leather came into the hands of scholars. Of the eleven, five were purchased by the Syrian Orthodox Convent of St. Mark in Jerusalem, and the remaining six by the Hebrew University of Jerusalem. The Syrian-owned scrolls were studied, photographed and partly published by scholars of the American Schools of Oriental Research. For a time they were deposited in a bank in New York, but at the beginning of 1955 they were sold to Israel for 250,000 dollars.

144

All the eleven scrolls will be permanently exhibited in a special hall in Jerusalem, to be called the Shrine of the Book.

THE ELEVEN MAIN MSS.

Of the Hebrew University MSS., four are part of one extremely interesting book, to which the late Prof. Sukenik gave the name *megillath ha-hodayoth*, or "Scroll of Thanks-givings". It consists of large sheets, each one folded, unlike the other manuscripts, which are in rolls. All told, there are twelve large columns, plus a great number of fragments. The text contains beautiful hymns which are very reminiscent of the Psalms in content, though entirely different in style.

Another of Sukenik's scrolls describes a probably purely allegorical war between "The Children of Light and the Children of Darkness"; it contains nineteen columns, written in an elegant Hebrew handwriting, the clearest of all the scrolls.

Finally, there is a second, but fragmentary, copy of the Book of Isaiah, known as *Isaiah Scroll B*. With a few minor exceptions, this text, unlike *Isaiah A*, follows the spelling of the Massoretic text.

Isaiah A, the largest and most sensational of all the scrolls, contains in its fifty-four columns the complete text, save for some *lacunae*, of the Book of Isaiah. The whole scroll was originally made by sewing together, with thread, seventeen sheets of somewhat coarse parchment or, rather, carefully prepared leather approaching the refinement of parchment. The sheets were carefully scored with a semi-sharp instrument. The lines were used as a guide for the tops of the letters, the letters being suspended from the lines, except that the *lamedh* naturally projects above the line.

The beautifully preserved writing averages twenty-nine lines to the column. The script belongs to the oldest type of Square Hebrew, and this scroll is, or at least seems to be, both the earliest of the whole group and the oldest existing major MS. of the Bible in any language. Notable features of *Isaiah A* are the particularly strange orthography (which also appears in other scrolls) and the fact that it agrees to a remarkable degree with the Massoretic text.

The *Sectarian Document*, also known as the "Covenant Scroll" or the "Manual of Discipline", is the next largest scroll in the group. It contains eleven columns of writing, with an average of twenty-six lines to the column. The script is

145

more recent than that of *Isaiah A*, and many of its letters (*'aleph, gimel, waw, lamedh, mem, nun, 'ayin, pe, qoph,* and *taw*) have an affinity with the graffiti on the ossuaries, but the difference of writing-material and of writing-tools must be taken into account. This scroll describes the initiation rites and oaths of allegiance of a monastic, Bible-centered community sect, which many scholars have identified with the Essenes, others with Judaeo-Christians, and others with other Jewish sects.

The Habakkuk Commentary deals with the first two chapters of the Book of Habakkuk. A short passage is taken from the Biblical text, and there follows a sort of commentary on contemporary conditions. The scroll consists of two pieces sewed together, each about five feet long. Apparently several lines are missing from the bottom of each column. The writing, different from that of the other MSS., is remarkably clear, large and regular. It is a rare, triangular style, though previously not altogether unknown. As in other scrolls, the letters are suspended from the lines. The most striking feature of this scroll is the use in several places of Early Hebrew letters, though in a stylized form, for writing the *Tetragrammaton* (see p. 82 f.).

Another scroll in this group, which, being the most brittle of all the scrolls, was not unrolled until 1956, was first thought to be the Aramaic apocryphal book of Lamech, but turned out to be a charming Aramaic *midrash* on *Genesis* with many stories and legends interwoven into the text. It is in a neat and fine style of Square Hebrew writing.

LATER DISCOVERIES

Early in 1949, Mr. G. Lankester Harding, then head of the Jordanian Department of Antiquities, and Père de Vaux, Head of the French Biblical and Archaeological School of Jerusalem, explored Qumran Cave 1 thoroughly and found some hundreds of fragments varying in size from ¼ inch to a third of a roll, and also some inscribed fragments of papyrus, written in some cases on both sides. Even more important was the discovery of the fragments written in the Early Hebrew script, referred to on p. 81 f.

In the spring of 1952, Père de Vaux and Prof. W. L. Reed, of the American School of Oriental Research in Jerusalem, discovered more inscribed fragments in Qumran Cave 2, a short distance south of Cave 1, and Cave 3, about one mile north of Cave 1. The most important find in Cave 3 was that of two inscribed copper scrolls, lying one upon the other, against the wall of the cave near the entrance (see p. 141).

In 1952, various explorations, some of them clandestine, were carried out in the immediate vicinity of Khirbet Qumran, particularly in the plateau between the cliffs and the Dead Sea. These have shown that every cave and rock shelter in the vicinity was utilized in some way. Unfortunately, the large natural caves have been used by Bedouin shepherds through the centuries, so that archaeological evidence there is very meagre. However, many more manuscripts have been discovered in what are now known as Qumran Caves 4, 5 and 6. Altogether, 230 unsuccessful soundings of caves were made, and pottery and other objects were found in thirty-nine caves and rock-shelters.

The manuscript-finds from Qumran Cave 4 surpass all the rest in interest and importance. Most of the manuscripts and fragments came into the hands of the Bedouins before the official excavation was carried out, but the Palestine Archaeological Museum and other Institutions, such as the University of Manchester, succeeded in acquiring from them some of the material, though this has not yet been delivered. At any rate, it is assumed that Qumran Cave 4 yielded more than four hundred Biblical MSS. (in thousands of tiny fragments, some not bigger than a stamp), including every book of the Hebrew Bible with the exception of the Book of Esther. There are several Isaiah MSS., and also various copies of the Pentateuch, Jeremiah, Psalms, and Daniel. There are also numerous fragments from Hebrew and Aramaic Apocrypha, non-canonical books such as Tobit, Jubilees, and Enoch, paraphrases of Biblical books, commentaries on Isaiah, the Psalms, and Malachi, phylacteries, liturgical texts, and hundreds of fragments of hitherto unknown works, which testify to the vast amount of literature composed in the last centuries before, and the first centuries of, the Christian era.

Of unique importance are fragments written in the Early Hebrew script, which represent—it would seem—about half a dozen books.

MANUSCRIPT-DISCOVERIES AT KHIRBET MIRD AND IN THE WADY MURABA'AT

In July 1952, clandestine exploration of an underground chamber at Khirbet al-Mird—a monastery ruin on a high peak about four miles north-east of the Greek Monastery of Mar Saba, and about nine miles south-east of Jerusalem—resulted in the discovery of a considerable number of Greek uncial and cursive documents of the fifth–eighth centuries C.E., of extremely interesting Palestinian–Syriac literary fragments and current papyri, and of Arabic papyri from the early Islamic period. A Belgian exploration of early 1953 found further Greek, Syriac, and Arabic fragments.

Wady Muraba'at, also known as Wady Darajeh, is a great gorge over 600 feet deep, almost sheer on its north side and steeply sloping on the south, lying in one of the most inaccessible districts of Palestine, some six to seven hours walk southeast from Bethlehem. Four natural caves were discovered here on the north side of the gorge, three of them together in a vertical rock face, the fourth on the slope above. Caves 1 and 2 are the largest—they are each over 150 feet long—and produced extremely significant manuscript fragments.

The history of the caves is as fantastic as the history of their discovery. When on 21st January, 1952, the expedition of the Jordan Department of Antiquities, the Archaeological Museum of Palestine, and the French Biblical School of Jerusalem arrived, they found thirty-four Arabs busy working by the light of small open paraffin flares. The excavators soon realized that there had also been earlier disturbances of the caves. A careful examination showed that the caves were inhabited at various times from the Chalcolithic period onwards (late fifth millennium B.C.E.). Chief interest, however, centered on the unique papyrus and leather inscribed documents, though the majority of them were torn to pieces and used as lining for rats' nests.

One of the most important and probably the oldest documents, was a papyrus palimpsest, that is, a papyrus from which the original writing had been washed or scraped off and then the papyrus re-used. While parchment palimpsests were quite frequently used in the Middle Ages, papyrus palimpsests were rare. Moreover, the importance of the present palimpsest is enhanced by the fact that the original text, which, of course, was not entirely erased, is written in the Early Hebrew script, not yet deciphered, but assigned by some scholars to the sixth century B.C.E., whereas the superimposed text is in Square Hebrew, containing a list of names with numerical signs.

There are also fifteen Greek and Square Hebrew ostraca, some containing only a few letters or a name; one large ostracon contains the first part of the Hebrew alphabet, each letter being written twice; and a longer text, of twelve incomplete lines, is written on three ostraca. There are various Greek papyrus documents, including one dated to 124 C.E. and one to 171 C.E. A Latin document in minuscule writing of the second century C.E. has also been found. The finds include relatively few, and badly mutilated, Biblical fragments, including passages from *Genesis, Exodus, Deuteronomy* and *Isaiah*, all agreeing with the Massoretic traditions; a phylactery, and a *Shema'* on another piece of the same parchment and in the same neat and minuscule script.

More important and indeed rather sensational, are Hebrew literary texts on papyrus from the period of the Bar Kochba war (132–135 C.E.), referring to "the deliverance of Israel by the ministry of Simeon ben Kosiba, Prince of Israel". No less important are two letters from Simeon ben Kosiba, that is Bar Kochba, to Yoshua' ben Galgola, the commander in Muraba'at. Also addressed to Yoshua' is a letter from two administrators of the village of Beth Mashko.

Of great interest, too, are some fragments in a cursive script, perhaps a cursive Hebrew or a cursive Nabataean, as yet not satisfactorily deciphered, though an excellent attempt at decipherment has been made by Dr. S. A. Birnbaum.

STILL MORE CAVES

Clandestine finds in three other caves of uncertain location were reported in 1952 and 1953. They include various Biblical texts in Greek, Biblical fragments in Square Hebrew and also a Hebrew letter to Simeon ben Kosiba; two Jewish documents in Aramaic, dated to the "third year of the liberation of Israel"; and several Greek and Aramaic cursive documents and cursive Nabataean papyri.

P.S.—The search for new caves and new scrolls goes on, but it is now a monopoly of clandestine (or shall we say "amateur") excavators, namely Bedouins. Quite recently, a new cave is supposed to have been discovered, which is tentatively called Cave 11, where apparently new scrolls have come to light, including copies of the *Psalms* and *Leviticus*, an "apocalyptic description of the New Jerusalem" and an "Aramaic *targum* of the Book of Job". In the meantime,

149

because of the political situation, the "Scrollery" of the Palestine Archaeological Museum in Jerusalem (now under Jordanian control) has been closed; the MS. fragments have been packed away in 36 cases and locked up in the Ottoman Bank of Amman, the capital of Jordan: let us hope that the brittle fragments will not rot away! The Western institutions who bought certain MSS. cannot receive them; neither can they have their money back. It goes without saying that the direct examination of the MSS. and the delicate process of restoration are at a standstill.

SIGNIFICANCE OF THE SCROLLS

The importance of all these scrolls cannot be over-estimated. We have acquired a new wealth of data for the study of Hebrew epigraphy and palaeography, philology, lexicography, grammar and syntax, liturgy and history, Bible and theology.

Although some manuscripts have been published, and also some fragments of unusual significance, it will take many years to assemble and prepare for publication the whole wealth of this manuscript material. Strictly speaking, only then shall we be able to assess the full value of the finds. This, needless to say, does not mean that in the meantime we should ignore the provisional results of the study of both published and unpublished material. At present, however, it is unwise to be dogmatic regarding any theory which has been propounded.

The essential chronological controversy whether the documents are to be dated to the first century B.C.E. or the first century C.E. is not of particular consequence. The fact is that, quite unexpectedly, we have now hundreds of Hebrew literary and cursive documents written in a beautiful book-hand, or rather in several book-hands, and in current styles.

The Muraba'at finds are of paramount historical importance, since in the absence of other literary sources they present us with what are unique glimpses of the administrative set-up of the Jewish forces in the unsuccessful attempt to overthrow the powerful Roman overlords. While they also furnish personal documents belonging to the legendary Bar Kochba, and varied evidence of the high cultural level of his military personel and of common folk, they also give us valuable chronological assistance and confirm the manuscript-dating obtained on palaeographical grounds.

CHAPTER 3

VOCALIZATION AND OTHER PUNCTUATION

THE HEBREW ALPHABET, as we have said, consists of the ancient twenty-two Semitic letters which are all consonants, though four of them (*'aleph, he, waw,* and *yodh*) are also used to represent long vowels, particularly at the end of a word. In Prof. Chomsky's opinion, these four letters, which originally were used consistently as consonants, began gradually to lose their weak consonantal value and became silent; eventually in some instances they were utilized as the so-called long vowels.

MATRES LECTIONIS

These letters have sometimes been called "vowel-letters" or "vocalic consonants", but are usually known as *matres lectionis,* "mothers of reading", because of their function to assist in reading; however, they are neither sufficient nor precise enough. In the first place, most of the vowels are not indicated at all; in the second place, one and the same *mater lectionis* is used for two or more vowel-sounds, and the same vowel-sound may be represented by various *matres lectionis.* Indeed, the letters *'aleph, he* and *'ayin* may be used in particular instances to represent any one of the vowel-sounds *â, ô, ê;* the *waw* may represent the vowel-sound *û* or *ô;* the *yodh,* the vowel-sounds *ê* or *î.* Although they may also function as long vowels these letters have remained consonants.

The insertion of the *matres lectionis* gives what is known as the *scriptio plena* ("full script"), their omission the *scriptio defectiva* ("defective script"). The date of origin of the *matres lectionis* is uncertain, but their introduction must have been gradual. It has been suggested that the first step in this direction was the need to indicate the sound of a long vowel when it formed the final sound of the word after having lost a consonant or even a syllable. Apparently, the first consonant employed in this manner was the *he* as an indication of a

151

final *ō*; later it was also used for final *ā* and *ē*; the *waw* was employed for final *ô* and *û*, the *yodh* for *ê* and *î*, and so on.

ABSENCE OF VOWEL-LETTERS

The absence of vowel-letters was not very strongly felt in Hebrew any more than it was in the other Semitic languages: see p. 39. On the other hand, as Hebrew speech passed out of daily use, and familiarity with Biblical Hebrew steadily declined—at least among the common people—it became necessary to introduce some form of vocalic distinction so that the *Torah* could be read and explained correctly. At the same time, no change in spelling or addition of letters was permitted: "The omission or the addition of one letter might mean the destruction of the whole world", says the *Talmud*.

Therefore, the textual orthography had to remain unchanged and such devices of vocalization had to be invented as were too insignificant to infringe the prohibition against change.

We do not know how far this injunction was observed in early times in manuscripts not destined for public service. At any rate it has always been strictly kept in the *Torah*-scrolls and, at least from post-Talmudic times, also in private codices.

UNUSUAL ORTHOGRAPHY

It is now known, however, that the injunction not to change orthography was not always strictly observed, at least by certain sects such as those of the Dead Sea Scrolls. Indeed, if we assume that they belong to the non-"Orthodox" category, it really would not matter.

At any rate, in the scroll *Isaiah A* we find: *wybw'* (instead of *wyb'* of the Massoretic text), xxvi. 2; *'wshqh* (instead of *'shqh*), xxxviii. 14; *'mtkh* (instead of *'mtk*), xxxviii. 19; *lw'* (instead of *l'*), xli. 7, lviii. 4 (twice), lxii. 6, etc.; *kwh* (instead of *kh*), xlix. 7; *wtw'rw* (instead of *wt'rw*), lii. 14; *mk'wbwt* (instead of *mk'bwt*), liii. 3; *ltbwh* (instead of *ltbh*), liii. 7; *lwqh* (instead of *lqh*), liii. 8; *rw'shw* (instead of *r'shw*), lviii. 5; *'wzw* (instead of *'zw*), lxii. 8; *'wzr* (instead of *'zr*), lxiii. 5; *w'bwsh* (instead of *w'bws*), lxiii. 6; *w'wrydh* (instead of *w'wryd*), *ib.*; *hmh* (instead of *hm*), lxv. 24; *wnk'y* (instead of *wnkh*), lxvi. 2; *hgw'ym* (instead of *hgwym*), lxvi. 20; and many other additions of vocalic-consonantal letters.

152

Whatever may be the situation, the ambiguity of a writing without vowels must have become more and more troublesome; and as there was thus a danger that the correct pronunciation might be finally lost, a system had to be devised to fix the exact pronunciation.

Although there is no historical account of the invention of such systems of vocalization, we may at least infer from other historical facts, that it was gradually developed in the Jewish schools of the early Christian centuries, perhaps under the influence of other schools, such as the Syrian. The pronunciation followed is probably in the main that of the Palestinian Jews of the third to sixth centuries C.E., as observed in the solemn reading of the *Torah* in synagogue and school, and partly based on a much older tradition. How far this tradition goes back, is very difficult to say. Some scholars doubt whether the real pronunciation of Early Hebrew was consistently preserved by Jewish tradition, especially in view of the transcription of proper names in the Septuagint, but quite often the accuracy of the Septuagint transliteration has been exaggerated. At any rate, in numerous cases, internal reasons as well as the analogy of allied languages, testify to the great faithfulness of the tradition.

WORK OF THE MASSORETES

On the other hand, there is the possibility that as in early times the Scriptures did not have the holy character they came to possess later, they may have been less carefully handled, and that less care was taken in copying them than in later times. A new epoch commenced during the First Exile, when the Scriptures were given to canonical status, and Holy Writings were venerated and handled with ever increasing care and conscientiousness.

This veneration was not given at once to all Biblical writings, but it certainly was accorded to the *Torah* (see also p. 167 ff.). The epoch of consolidation probably begins with Ezra and extends to the close of the Talmud, about 500 C.E.: it thus lasted nearly a millennium. During this long period, the whole text was fixed together with its exact pronunciation. Indeed, the development of the pronunciation and, needless to say, of vocalization, kept pace with the settlement of the text.

153

During this entire period down to the close of the *Talmud*, the Sacred text was without vowels or other points. The Massoretic system of punctuation is of later origin, but this does not mean that during the same period the *reading* of the text was still unsettled among the Jews; it must rather be assumed that with the official fixing of the text there also developed a certain mode of understanding and of reading it. The *Talmud*—to judge from the agreement of its Biblical quotations with the Massoretic text—gives the Text throughout correctly. We have therefore to assume that long before the Massoretes the pronunciation was fixed, though not yet written, and that it was handed down by word of mouth; it is possible that some scholars may have used signs in their note-books to assist their memory.

In the course of time, however, means had to be adopted by Jewish grammarians for the permanent preservation of the traditional pronunciation of every word and letter, by attaching to the consonants certain signs representing the proper sounds. Their labor shows a thorough and correct understanding of the Sacred text; extraordinary pains were taken to perpetuate it in its purity.

Accordingly there came into being the various systems of punctuation, which developed more or less independently but in a parallel manner in the Eastern Academies of Babylonia and the Western Academies of Palestine (e.g., at Tiberias): see also p. 155ff. From the Persian period onwards, the *Sopherim*, or "literati", successors of Ezra, began to accumulate all the notes on the Biblical text, and their work was continued at intervals by the rabbis after the fall of Jerusalem.

The late Dr. Gaster ascribed to the ancient *Sopherim* the preservation of the ancient traditional pronunciation of Hebrew, the preservation of the text of the *Torah* in its accuracy down to the most minute details, such as the separating of the words, the arrangements of the sections, also the full and defective writing, with its anomalies and archaisms, and the creation of the tittles (see p. 168 f.).

The copious notes, largely oral—though partly of course written—were transmitted and elaborated in the Academies, and later written down as *Massoreth* or *Massorah*, "tradition"; the term probably derives from a root *msr*, "to hand on". It has been suggested that with the earlier Massoretes, fifth to eighth centuries C.E., *Massoreth* was equivalent to orthography,

154

that is *plene* and *defective* writing (see p. 151), and only later came to mean "tradition". It is impossible to construct an unbroken history of the Massoretes or of the progress of their work, but the marginal notes in ancient Biblical codices, as well as the fragments of other works show that the work of some of the later Massoretes can be traced back to the eighth century C.E.

Anxiously following in the footsteps of the older grammarians in their efforts to fix and guard the traditional text, they laid down more minute grammatical and linguistic rules, and in this respect a great part of the contents of the *Massorah* is new. They fixed the reading of the text; its vowel-marks, accents, signs which affect the reading of the consonants, such as *dagesh*, *mappîq*, *raphe*, the diacritical points to *shin*, and so on. This patient and learned labor came to an end in the tenth century C.E.; and from then onwards, copies of the Hebrew Scriptures, and particularly those intended for public use, followed the detailed prescriptions of the *Massorah*.

In 1525, the famous Bomberg press in Venice, under the supervision of the learned Jakob ben Ḥayyim, printed the whole Hebrew Bible with commentaries, strictly based on the prescriptions of the *Massorah*.

MAIN SYSTEMS OF PUNCTUATION
(VOCALIZATION)

Until about a century ago, only the Tiberias vocalization system was known. Since then, other systems have come to light. It is thought that they are the records of different schools, or the preserved variations in pronunciation of different localities.

The three main vowel systems now extant are the "Babylonian", the "Palestinian", and the "Tiberiadic" or "Tiberian". In Prof. Max Weinreich's opinion, these vowel systems corresponded with three regional systems of pronouncing the vowels, the Northwestern, Southwestern, and Eastern. The Babylonian Academies, then the foremost centers of Jewish learning, were the focus of the Eastern region, which extended to the frontiers of India and China and southward to the Yemen. The Southwestern region included Southern Palestine and the southern shores of the Mediterranean as far as the Atlantic. The Northwestern pronunciation, favored and

155

standardized but not necessarily created by the Tiberias school, was in vogue in Northern Palestine, Syria, and in the adjacent Byzantine territory.

BABYLONIAN SYSTEM

The Babylonian is a "superlinear" system of both vocalization and accentuation; its main characteristic feature is the representation of vowel-sounds by small additional letters, the letter *'aleph* for long *a*, *'ayin* for short *a*, *waw* for *u*, and *yodh* for *i*, double *yodh* for long *e*, and double *waw* for long *o*. These small letters, except the *waw*, and some other graphic signs were placed above the consonants, leaving the textual orthography unchanged.

The Babylonian system is preserved in a number of Biblical manuscripts and fragments most of which were discovered in ancient synagogues at Chufutkale, Karasubazar, and Theodosia, in the Crimea. Although this system (the *niqqûd bavlî*, "Babylonian punctuation") has been known to Western scholars since 1846, a more thorough study of it was made possible only in 1876 when a facsimile of the famous Leningrad *Prophet-codex* of the year 916 was published by Prof. H. Strack. This precious codex was discovered by Firkowitch in 1839 in the synagogue at Chufuktale, in the Crimea.

The Babylonian vocalic system differs from the Tiberian almost throughout in form, and partly also in the sounds of the marks, whereas the accents are fairly similar and in some cases are under the line of the consonants. In the *Targum*, the Aramaic version, a simpler system was used. While, according to some scholars, the Babylonian system was an independent Eastern creation contemporaneous with the Western, or Tiberian, according to others it was a later, and not altogether successful, attempt to modify and simplify the Western system, originally common both to the Western and the Eastern schools.

PALESTINIAN SYSTEM

The Palestinian system was also "superlinear", but its basic element was the dot. The varying position, as well as the change in the arrangement and in the number of the dots, determined the value of the vowel-sound. The Palestinian vowel-system is preserved only in some fragmentary manuscripts discovered, since the end of the last century, in the Cairo *Genizah*. They

156

contain very small fragments of Biblical codices, but a greater number of liturgical texts and *Targumîm* with Biblical passages. See also p. 142.

At first, scholars thought that this was "a strange form of Hebrew shorthand accompanied by a new kind of vocalization". It is now commonly agreed that it is the "Palestinian" system of vocalization, which was the oldest of the three systems and probably formed the basis of the other two. Prof. Kahle has subdivided the Palestinian system into three groups, two being similar to the Tiberian, and one to the Babylonian system. The texts with Palestinian vocalization contain numerous abbreviations.

Apparently, the "Palestinian" pronunciation was based on five vowels only, corresponding to the Latin or Continental vowel-sounds *a, e, i, o, u*; thus, the vowel-mark *a* corresponded to the "Tiberian" *pathaḥ* and *qamaṣ*, except for the *qamaṣ qaṭon*, and the vowel-mark *e* corresponded to the "Tiberian" *seghol* and *ṣerê*.

TIBERIAN SYSTEM

The Tiberian or "Tiberiadic" system, which is the one with which most of our readers will be familiar, is partly "superlinear", but mainly "sublinear". It consists of dots and little dashes, and denotes also semi-vowels. It is, indeed, a highly developed system and far more precise and comprehensive than the others. It has seven notation marks, though these represent more vowel-sounds (see p. 183ff.): *qamaṣ* for the sound *a–o*, *pathaḥ* for the sound *a*, *segēl* or *seghôl* for the sound *e*, *ḥireq* for the sound *i*, or rather *ee*, *shûreq* (*waw* with a dot to the left) for long *u* or *oo*, *qibbuṣ* for *u* or *oo*, *ḥolêm* (*waw* with a dot on top) for long *o*, *ṣere* for long *e*, and *shewâ* for a semi-vowel which can be used either independently or in connection with another vocalic notation mark. For a certain period only seven main vowels (*shibhâh melakhîm*, "seven kings") were counted, which Elias Levita indicates by the mnemonic *wayomer 'Eliyahû* ("And Elijah said"); *shûreq* and *qibbuṣ* were counted as one vowel. See also p. 185.

Apart from the vocalization marks, there are the Tiberian notation marks which regularly indicate the word-tone and secondary stresses (see p. 159ff.).

The Tiberian punctuation finally gained general acceptance, while the others gradually fell into oblivion. As its main element is the dot, the Tiberian system was probably considered far too insignificant to infringe the prohibition of change in traditional orthography.

ORIGIN OF THE PUNCTUATION-SYSTEMS

The origin of the Hebrew notation-mark systems, and particularly the date or dates of their invention are still uncertain. While according to some scholars, all the Hebrew systems were based on the Nestorian dot system and were thus, in origin, later than 750 C.E., according to others, the process of establishing the Hebrew vocalic notation system was gradual and of very long duration. The latter view is probably correct; furthermore, these systems of punctuation may have gone through several stages in their evolution.

However, it is probable that Hebrew and Syriac influenced each other in this respect. In the Syriac scripts, three main vowel systems developed in the seventh and eighth centuries C.E. The earliest, but less complete, was the Nestorian system; it consisted partly of a combination of the consonants *w* and *y* and a dot placed above or below, and partly of one or two dots placed above or, mainly, below the consonant to be vocalized.

The Jacobite system, created about 700 C.E., was more complete; it consisted of small Greek letters placed above or below the line. Finally, the late West Syrian system consisted of a combination of the diacritical vowel marks and the small Greek letters. The Hebrew systems do not resemble any of them and are partly earlier than all of those, but there may have been what is now known as *idea-diffusion* or *stimulus-diffusion*, that is of the borrowing simply of an *idea*, in which case it will never be possible to prove either way, not even a "mutual influence".

However, it is generally held that the Palestinian system, which is the earliest (see p. 156 f.), was employed from the sixth century C.E. onwards. The Babylonian system was evolved in the famous Jewish Academies which flourished in Mesopotamia from the third to the tenth centuries C.E. Prof. Kahle has suggested that in Nisibis (N. Mesopotamia) a Jewish Academy was active in the sixth century, and that its studies may have been influenced by the celebrated Nestorian school in that city,

158

founded in the early fifth century C.E. Finally, the Tiberian system was definitely fixed in the late eighth century C.E.; in the following two centuries it became the common classical Hebrew punctuation system, known as *niqqûd.*

Then, as we read in contemporary sources, teachers went out from Tiberias to far-away countries, such as Babylonia and Persia, to instruct in the "Palestinian" way of reading Hebrew. According to Prof. Weinreich, however, with the rise and the expansion of the Arabs, impoverished Palestine was reduced to a modest secondary role and the Talmudic schools of Babylonia became preponderant.

Around the middle of the eleventh century, adversity befell the Babylonian Gaonate too, and the dependence of its far-famed Academies upon outside financial support became greater than ever. Driven by necessity, scholars had to emigrate in growing numbers, and when eventually the Academy closed down altogether, most of the scholars had to emigrate. As, however, Weinreich argues, the precarious state of the Babylonian center of learning resulted in what is comparable to the exodus of Greek scholars from Constantinople after the city had fallen to the Turks (in 1453), along with the Jewish settlements east and south of Babylonia, Ashkenaz was to gain by what Babylonia lost.

At any rate, by the twelfth century the Tiberian pointing system had gained general acceptance to the exclusion of the other systems.

ACCENTS OR WORD-TONES AND STOPS

In the Biblical vocalized texts, each word has an accent. There are about thirty accents and they form a very elaborate and complicated system, these small signs being generally placed above or below the consonants, and sometimes between them.

The accents have three uses:

(1) To mark the tone-syllable of a word, that is, to indicate the syllable to be stressed in pronunciation; in this sense, the accent is the guide to the pronunciation of the individual word.

(2) As marks of interpunctuation, the accents indicate the logical or syntactical relation of single words to the whole sentence; in this sense, the accents are of two kinds—distinctive, that is marks which separate, like our commas and stops, and conjunctive or continuation marks; the former mark out the

main sections of a sentence, the latter indicate the connections between the minor parts.

The two major stops are called (*a*) *sillûq*, meaning "end", which always appears under the last word of a verse, and is regularly followed by a sign called *sôph pasûq*, "end of the verse", and (*b*) *'athnāḥ*, "rest", which divides the verse into two logical parts. Each of these parts is divided by other marks into two further parts, and so on. The system of these accents varies according to the Biblical texts: the system in the poetical books—*Psalms*, *Proverbs*, and also *Job*—is somewhat different from that of the other books.

(3) To signify the pitch or tone of the voice, that is as musical signs, in the cantillation of the Scriptures in the Synagogue; in this sense—which of course embraces the other two—the accents are guides to the proper reading of the text as a whole, which is a kind of recitation or chanting.

According to some scholars, the majority of the accents were adopted from the Greek neums, a sort of musical notation, and punctuation marks, and, like these, their primary purpose was to regulate the public reading of the Sacred text down to the smallest detail. The gradual change from the speaking voice in public reading to chanting or singing, caused the Jews to forget the real origin of the system, which became completely transformed and amplified into the three classes as shown above.

DAGESH AND OTHER DIACRITICAL MARKS

Of the other diacritical marks, special mention must be made of the use of the *dagesh* (see also p. 178), that is a dot in the consonants *beth*, *gimel*, *daleth*, *kaph*, *pe*, and *taw*, to harden or double their sounds, this being known as the *dagesh qal*—a term first employed by the grammarian David Qimhi—or *lene*, or in other consonants, to double their sounds, this being the *dagesh forte*, or "strong".

Scholars differ as to the origin of the *dagesh*. According to Prof. Tur-Sinai, the *dagesh lene* was the original *dagesh* and it served exclusively to mark the hard pronunciation of the letters *b–g–d k–p–t*. Since this *dagesh* also occurred after a short vowel, in which case the consonants were hardened or doubled, the use of the *dagesh* was extended by the grammarians and is was also used as *dagesh forte*. In Prof. Chomsky's opinion, however, the *dagesh* is to be traced back to the pre-vocalic

160

stage. In its original use, according to Chomsky it indicated that the consonant had a vowel, while the *raphe*-mark—a horizontal stroke above the consonant—indicated a vowel-less pronunciation of the consonant. The invention of these diacritical marks—which appear in the earliest dated Hebrew MS., the Leningrad Prophet-codex of 916—is attributed to the Rabbis, who, it is thought, wished to guard their public against mispronunciation.

Prof. Chomsky's theory seems to be correct. It is interesting to note that, for instance, in the Deva-nagari, the script of the Sanskrit language, an oblique stroke, called *virama*, is sometimes placed below the consonant to indicate that it is vowelless; furthermore, in Arabic vocalized texts consonants provided with the sign *sukun* are vowel-less. By analogy, although by a different procedure, in some old Hebrew manuscripts we find a *dagesh* mark in all letters following pure consonants.

Thus, apparently, the original main purpose of the *dagesh* must have been to indicate that the preceding consonant was to be pronounced without a vowel. With the introduction, however, of the vocalic notation-marks, the *sheva* may have been regarded as sufficient indication of vowel-less consonants. Therefore, the *dagesh* was inserted only in the letters *b–g–d k–p–t*, to denote the change of pronunciation of these characters, and after the letters *aleph, he, heth, 'ayin* to indicate that they have not to be pronounced with a vocalic or semivocalic value.

The *mappîq* (a sign which brings out the sound "distinctly", i.e. as a consonant) is a point which when inserted in the letters *he, waw, yodh*, or above the *'aleph*, indicates that these letters preserve their consonant force instead of quiescing as they generally do at the end of a word. The *mappîq* is mainly used in the consonantal *he* at the end of a word, since this letter can never be a vowel in the middle of a word. According to some scholars the *he* with a *mappîq* was distinctly aspirated like the Arabic *hâ* at the end of a syllable.

Another interesting diacritic mark must be mentioned. It is highly probable that in ancient times the pronunciation of the letter *shin* was constant. In the course of time, however, two different pronunciations have developed: *sh* and *s*. When the Massoretes fixed the definite arrangement of the vocalic notation marks, they also tried to define the exact pronunciation of the consonants. In order to distinguish the two variants in the pronunciation of the letter *shin*, a dot was introduced to be placed above this letter, to the left or to the right, to differentiate the sound *s* from *sh* (see also p. 36).

PRONUNCIATION OF *b–g–d k–ph–t*

We have frequently referred to the constancy of pronunciation of the Hebrew letters. The exception is the double pronunciation—not yet satisfactorily explained—of the letter *shin*, and also of the letters *b–g–d k–p–t*.

Prof. Tur-Sinai has suggested a plausible theory for the history of the pronunciation of the latter group. He proved that the letters *b–g–d k–p–t* passed through three evolutionary stages. Originally they were all pronounced hard, that is as plosives, even when preceded by a vowel.

During the period of the Second Commonwealth, however, the letters *b–g–d* were consistently pronounced hard, while the letters *k–p–t* were just as consistently pronounced soft. This change, in Prof. Tur-Sinai's opinion, was due to the influence of the Babylonian pronunciation of these letters. Finally, the pronunciation now commonly used in the reading of the *Torah* was fixed by the early *naqdanîm*—see further on.

ACCURATE NOTATION

All these diacritic or punctuation marks are due mainly to a long course of grammatical refinement made by the Massoretes. Thanks to their efforts we are now furnished with an extremely accurate notation for the Hebrew language. Punctuation marks, however, were not to be employed in the synagogue scrolls, but were always to be used in Biblical codices, later also in the printing of the Bible.

NAQDANÎM

It may be pointed out that "punctuation", including of course vocalization, assumed paramount importance in the instruction given in the Jewish Academies in the post-Talmudic era. Several Biblical codices written before the fifteenth century contain two colophons, one giving the name of the scribe, the other of the *naqdan*, "punctuator" or vocalizer. A colophon is the final paragraph of a codex and generally gives the name of the copyist and the date and place of production, pious remarks being frequently added; not all codices, however,

162

have colophons, and most colophons do not give full information.

The qualifications of the scribe, or *sopher*, were quite different from those of the *naqdan*: the former had to be a first-class calligrapher and had to know all the rules and regulations for the preparation and copying of the *Sepher Torah*. The scribe, however, was not always an expert in *diyyûq*, or "accuracy" and "exactness", that is all the vast lore of the grammarians and Massoretes, the knowledge of which was indispensable for applying correctly to the text all the diacritical points of vocalization, accents, and so on. This was the work of the *naqdan*, whose task it was to bring the Biblical codex to completion. The specialization of the *naqdanim* in what we would now call philology and grammar also gave them the opportunity of supplementing these codices with the *massoretic* notes referred to on p. 153 ff. The main activity of the *naqdanim* started about 1000.

The *naqdanim* are not to be confused with the Massoretes, who were called by some Hebrew savants *ba'alê-haniqqûd*, the "owners", "knowers", or creators of the punctuation, who established the final text of the Sacred Scriptures by the institution of the vocalic marks, accents, and other diacritical signs (see p. 155 ff.). Nevertheless, it would be wrong to assume that the *naqdanim* limited their activity to the transcription of the *niqqûd* from earlier codices.

Indeed, they introduced numerous changes in detailed notes in order to render the pronunciation of the text more and more accurate. Hence, their great contribution in the field of pronunciation and grammar of the Hebrew language. The numerous variants in vocalic and other marks which occur in the different Biblical codices are partly to be attributed to the original activity of the *naqdanim*. The classical case of such discrepancies in the reading and pronunciation of the Sacred text is that of the codices attributed to the two most celebrated schools of *naqdanim* and grammarians, the Ben Asher school and the Ben Naphtali school, the rival-schools which flourished in the late ninth and the first half of the tenth century at Tiberias (see also p. 159).

Several *naqdanim* wrote treatises on the right pronunciation of the Sacred text and also on Hebrew grammar. These treatises cannot always be dated or attributed to individual scholars, but are frequently quoted in Biblical codices which have been preserved. We may refer to '*Ayin ha-Qorê*, "Eye of the Reader", by a certain Yequtiel b. Yehudah ha-Kohen *hanaqdan*, the *Miphteaḥ ha-diqdûq*, "Key of the Grammar", by a certain R. Shimshon *hanaqdan*, a *Sepher ha-Masorah*, "Book of the Massorah", a *Sha'arê ha-niqqûd*, "Gates of the Punctuation", *Darkê ha-niqqûd*, "Ways of the Punctuation", and so on. Very famous is the '*Eṭ Sopher*, "Pen of the Scribe", by the celebrated R. David Qimḥi.

Several names of *naqdanim* have been preserved, though after the second half of the fourteenth century the study of Hebrew grammar, *Massorah* and *niqqûd*, gradually declined, and very little is known of later *naqdanim*. But several fifteenth-century codices are extant, in which the scribe notes that he has written the codex and punctuated it.

164

CHAPTER 4

DEVELOPMENT OF THE SQUARE HEBREW SCRIPT

ITS EARLIEST TEACHING

THE SYSTEMATIC TEACHING of the Early Hebrew alphabet has been referred to on p. 64. Following the Babylonian conquest of Judaea and the deportation to Babylon of the Jewish leaders, the cultural level of the country sank considerably; see also p. 134. Not until we reach the first century B.C.E., or perhaps only in the first century C.E., can we assume that there was an organized school system in Judaea, and in such schools the reading of the Scrolls of the Bible would have been the main subject to be taught. Previously, teaching was done exclusively by fathers, and there are many Talmudic utterances which dwell upon the importance of the duty of fathers to teach their children and upon the value of the instruction of children in general. Very significant are such Talmudic verses as: "We may not suspend the instruction of children even for the rebuilding of the Temple" or "A city in which there are no schoolchildren will suffer destruction" (*Shabbath*, 119b).

NATIONAL SCHOOL SYSTEM

The first attempt at creating a school-system is attributed to Simeon b. Shetaḥ, about 65 B.C.E. (*Talm. Pal.*, *Kethuboth* viii. 11, 32c); but a comprehensive scheme was carried out by Joshua b. Gamala, about 63 C.E. (*Baba Bathra*, 21a). Joshua "instituted that teachers should be appointed in every province and in every city, and children about the age of six or seven placed in their charge". Dr. A. Cohen emphasized that this is probably the earliest record of national education in any country. The same Talmudic Tractate gives some ultra-modern advice: "The maximum number of elementary pupils that should be placed under one teacher, is twenty-five; if there are fifty, an additional teacher must be provided; if there are forty, a senior student should be engaged to assist the master".

MNEMONIC DEVICE FOR THE *ALEPH-BETH*
(See also p. 38)

Dr. A. Cohen draws our attention to an extremely interesting Talmudic passage, Tractate *Shabbath*, 104*a*, which informs us how the infants were taught the Hebrew *aleph-beth* with the aid of key-words used as mnemonic devices, and at the same time employed as a medium of religious and ethical instruction. How advanced these sages were over some modern scholars who still "recognize" the *'aleph* as "(head of an) ox", the *beth* as "house", the *gimel* as "camel", and so on (see also p. 39f.). Here is the passage.

"It is related that children now come into the House of Study who recite things the like of which was not even said in the days of Joshua the son of Nun. *'Aleph* and *beth* are the initials of two words meaning 'gain understanding'. *Gimel* and *daleth*: 'be benevolent to the poor'; why is the foot of *gimel* turned towards *daleth*? because it is the way of the benevolent to run after the poor; why is the foot of *daleth* turned towards *gimel*? to indicate that the poor person reaches out to his helper; why is the face of *daleth* turned away from *gimel*? to teach that charity should be performed in secret so as not to shame the recipient. *He* and *waw* signify the name of the Holy One, blessed be He. *Zayin*, *heth*, *teth*, *yodh*, *kaph*, *lamed*: if you act in this manner (towards the poor), the Holy One, blessed be He, will sustain you, be gracious to you, benefit you, give you an inheritance, and bind a crown upon you in the World to come. There is an open *mem* and a closed *mem*, denoting that certain doctrines are open to the reason and others closed. There is a curved *nun* and a straight *nun*, hinting that if one is faithful to God when bent (by adversity) he will be faithful in normal times. *Samekh* and *'ayin* provide two words meaning 'support the poor', or according to another version 'make mnemonics' when studying the *Torah* as an aid to retaining it in memory. There is a curved *pe* and a straight *pe*, pointing to an open mouth and a closed mouth. There is a curved *sade* and a straight *sade*, meaning that if one is righteous when bent (by adversity) he will be righteous in normal times. *Qoph* is the first letter of 'holy' and *resh* of 'wicked'; why

166

does *qoph* turn its face away from *resh*? the Holy One, blessed be He, says, 'I cannot look upon the wicked'; why is the foot of *qoph* turned towards *resh*? the Holy One, blessed be He, says, 'if the wicked repent, I will place a crown upon him like my own'; why does the leg of *qoph* hang detached? if the wicked repents he can enter through the opening (and so find himself within the Holy One). *Shin* is the initial of 'falsehood', and *taw* the final letter of 'truth'; why does the word for 'falsehood' consist of three consecutive letters of the alphabet while the word for 'truth' consists of letters taken from the beginning, middle, and end of the alphabet? because falsehood is common, truth uncommon; why does the word for falsehood rest on one point while the word for truth has a firm foundation? to teach that truth stands but falsehood does not stand."

SCROLL OF THE LAW—SYNAGOGUE SCROLL

"SEPHER TORAH"—TORAH-SCROLL

The main classification of Hebrew manuscripts is into scrolls and codices. The former are reserved for use in the public reading of the Synagogue worship. By Synagogue scrolls, we mean *Torah* (or "Pentateuch")-scrolls, though the *Book of Esther* is also read in the public worship of the Synagogue from a parchment scroll. The *Torah* is the original fountain of inspiration on which the later Biblical books and the Talmud drew. *Ps.* xl. 8 seems to support the Talmudic tradition that the Psalmist came into the Temple with the Scroll of the Law. On the Arch of Titus a scroll is being carried in the triumphal procession. The Tractate *Ta'anith* ("Fast") says that "the Romans, after the capture of Jerusalem, wrapped her school-children in their Scrolls and burnt them" (*Ta'anith*, 62a). It was an accepted dogma that the *Torah* was inspired by God. "He who says that the *Torah* is not from heaven, has no portion in the World to come" (*Sanhedrin* x. 1).

Nowadays, the Reading of the *Torah* is a main feature of the Synagogue service; every synagogue must contain at least one copy of such a scroll. The scrolls are put in the holy Ark—which is placed in that part of the building facing Jerusalem—before which burns a perpetual light.

The writing of the Scroll of the Law is a task requiring much

167

care, erudition, and labor. "It is a *halakhah* from Moses on Sinai to write on leather with ink and to rule (*sargal*) with a reed (*qaneh*)", we read in *Megill.* 71*d*, 9. The ink should be black and be prepared according to a definite recipe.

The model must be an authentic copy and the scribe must not deviate in the least from it. No word or letter, not even a *yodh*, must be written from memory: the scribe must copy it from the model before him. The space of a hair or thread must be left blank between each consonant; between each word the breadth of a narrow consonant; between each section, the breadth of nine consonants; between each book, three lines. The last line of the *Book of Deuteronomy* must be a complete line, but the last line of the other four books need not be.

The following regulations (*Treat. Sopherim* iv. 1–6) are very interesting: "The letter *bêth* in the first word of the *Torah*, *bereshith*, must have four *taggîn,* and the letters of this word must be written widely spread out, wider than any other, because by it the world was established. *Waw* of the word *gaḥôn* (*Lev.* xi. 42) must be standing up higher, because it marks the middle of the *Torah* by letters. The words *darosh* and *darash* (*Lev.* x. 16) must be so written that one line finishes with the first word and the next line begins with the second word, for this is the middle of the *Torah*. In the word *wayishḥaṭ* (*Lev.* viii. 23) the letter *ḥeth* must be spread out, because this is the middle of the verses of the *Torah*. The verse *shema' yisrael*, etc. (*Deut.* vi. 4) must occupy a line by itself. . . . *Yisrael,* the last word of the *Torah* (*Deut.* xxxiv. 12), must be written with all the letters spread out, and the *lamed* therein must be the longest of all the similar letters in the *Torah*."

The text is always written without the vowel-marks and other diacritic points, but is supplied with "tittles". According to some scholars these decorations on the tops of various consonants act as guides for pronunciation and are ancient; according to others, they are simply ornamental.

TAGGÎN (pl. of *tag*)

The "tittles", in Hebrew *taggîn* (or "crowns"), are also called *zainin* (explained either as the small letter *zayin* which they are made to resemble, or "weapons" such as small daggers) or *ṣiyunîm* ("marks" or "signs") or *qarnaya* (Aramaic term for "horns" or "sharp points"). The letters decorated

168

with *taggîn* were called *metuyagîm* or *mezuyanîm* or *meṣuyanîm*. These letters are not of a uniform character: some are twisted or turned, the *taggîn* being put above, at the sides, or below the letters, in an almost bewildering variety. The *taggîn*, moreover, sometimes assume the form of ringlets or curves above the letters, and twists inside them; but most of them are little strokes in varying numbers over the letters.

We find letters with one stroke, others with two or three, and some even with six. Often one letter is singled out for marking, on other occasions two or more, and not seldom every letter of the word is marked with a *tag*. Sometimes the number of strokes is the same for each of the letters, but frequently the number of the strokes varies. In some letters strokes are added on the right and on the left in addition to those on the top. All this is in the opinion of the late Dr. Gaster the result of a slow development, which starting probably with one single stroke or curve, multiplied.

The late Dr. Moses Gaster, *Hacham* of the Sephardic Communities in England, has dedicated to this subject a very interesting and learned monograph: *The Tittled Bible. A Model Codex of the Pentateuch*, London, 1929. Gaster emphasizes the great importance of the tittles and their antiquity, based on ancient quotations, such as *Exod. Rabba*, Sect. vi ("Solomon and a thousand like him shall pass away, but not a tittle of thee [the *Torah*] will I allow to be expunged"); *St. Matthew* v. 18 ("For verily I say unto you, Till heaven and earth pass away, one jot or one tittle shall in no wise pass away from the *Law*, etc."); and *St. Luke* xvi. 17 ("But it is easier for heaven and earth to pass away, than for one tittle of the *Torah* to fall"). He ascribes the creation of the "tittles" or "crowns" (*taggîn* or *iṭṭûr*) to the ancient *Sopherim*, referred to on p. 130 f.

Indeed, according to Gaster the *taggîn* were the earliest accents in the Hebrew script and were the result of the desire of the *Sopherim* to enable the people to understand the text of the *Torah* and the underlying intentions of the Divine legislation correctly. In his view the *taggîn* belong to the first phase in the development of Massoretic signs, whereas the accents and the vocalic marks (see p. 155 ff.) belong to the second and the third phases. And only the signs of the first phase (i.e. the *taggîn*) were within the rules of the preparation of the *Torah*-scroll.

169

MODEL CODICES FOR TORAH-SCROLLS

Dr. Gaster suggests that the Model Codices (called later *tiqqunîm*) mentioned in the ancient Massoretic notes to the Bible were not Massoretic codices with vowels and accents, but Model Codices for the *Torah*-scroll. No Scribe could start, indeed, from the Massoretic text, and undertake the enormous task of re-arranging the columns, lines, and words in such a manner as to copy it straight into his own Scroll, without making innumerable mistakes. Nor was any Scribe allowed to use another Scroll as a supplementary Model, from which to copy word by word and line by line. He must, therefore, have had before him a real model, a manuscript so arranged as to be in strict accordance with the old rules and traditions. Such Model Codices, however, were not sacred, and there was no harm in making notes in them or correcting them, or referring to other codices.

In Gaster's opinion, only one such Model Codex has been preserved, and is No. 85 of the Gaster Collection, now in the British Museum. It has been edited by Gaster (1929) in the work previously referred to. It is written in an Oriental hand, probably by the middle of the fourteenth century, on yellow Oriental paper. Two pages correspond to one column in the Scroll, each column containing fifty-two lines; each line contains the prescribed number of letters. It thus agrees, also in other respects, with the tradition mentioned by Maimonides. After the invention of printing, the scrolls were copied from printed Model Texts or *Tiqqunîm*.

The *Torah*-scrolls do not show a uniform tradition as to the tittles, their number, shape, and the words and letters upon which they are placed. Dr. Gaster distinguishes three such traditions: (1) that represented by the *Sepher Taggîn* ("Handbook of Tittles") referred to by Naḥmanides (1194–1267) and incorporated in the *Măḥazor Vitry* of the twelfth-century; (2) that of Menaḥem Meïri (Don Vidal of Perpignan, 1249–1306), incorporated in his *Qiryath Sepher*; and (3) that of the Model Codex already referred to.

DATING TORAH-SCROLLS

The script of the *Torah*-scrolls, always in the Square style, shows little change with the passing of the centuries. Moreover, as the science of dating this writing has not yet been put on a firm basis, the dates of the *Torah*-scrolls are very difficult to determine. It is not to be assumed, however, that all the Law-scrolls are uniform. Indeed, a careful examination would enable us to classify and group them. One of the criteria, suggested by Dr. Moses Gaster, could be the affinity or difference with one of the three tittle-traditions for which he contends. At any rate, their history belongs rather to a work on Hebrew palaeography than to one on the History of the Hebrew alphabet.

HEBREW BIBLICAL CODICES

In view of what has been said with regard to the *Torah*-scroll, it is evident that a History of the Hebrew alphabet should be concerned rather with manuscripts in codex-form than with ritual Synagogue-scrolls.

As far as the codices were concerned, there were no rules for their writing, no prescriptions for the preparation of the ink or the material on which the text was to be written; no rules about the distances between letters and words, between column and column, or the number of letters in each line of the column; no rules regarding erasure, supplying omissions, or eliminating dittographies, that is repetitions of identified words (or lines) in consecutive lines; nor anything concerning the writing of the Holy Name, corrections, a full or defective script; no rules prescribing the size or even the form of the letters. Hence, apart from the Square Hebrew type, Rabbinic script and even cursive hands were sometimes, though rarely, used in Biblical codices. Here and there, even ligatures of two letters are found. Parchment as well as paper may be used. No question is raised as to the religious character of the Scribe; no objection is made to ornamentation in gold and color, or to the use of gold in the writing of the letters. But the Biblical codex was never allowed to be used in the divine service for reading the lessons from the *Torah*, and can never replace the *Torah*-scroll. Having said all this, we must emphasize that the Biblical codex has always been treated in all respects as the most important of books, and the maximum care was always taken to make it conform as accurately as possible with the Massoretic traditions of one or another school of the Holy Land or of Babylonia.

It is difficult to say, even approximately, how many Hebrew

codices are extant, the more so since little information is available about certain important collections both public and private. We know little or nothing, for instance, about the contents of the Leningrad State Library, and other collections in the U.S.S.R., which is the repository of more important as well as of more numerous ancient Hebrew codices than any other country in the World.

The famous De' Rossi Collection in the Palatina Library at Parma in Northern Italy, is perhaps the richest in Biblical codices; it contains over 800 such MSS., though only few of them contain the whole Hebrew Bible. The total number of Hebrew Biblical codices extant amounts to over 3000. The oldest of them, ignoring the Dead Sea Scrolls, apparently belong to the ninth century C.E.

Making a very rough estimate, it may be assumed that, in all, some 30,000 Hebrew codices are extant, to which should be added many tens of thousands of fragmentary codices and other MS. fragments found in Oriental *Genizas* (see p. 142), in the Dead Sea Caves, and so on. The Library of the Jewish Theological Seminary of America (New York) has probably the richest Western collection of Hebrew MSS. Other rich American collections are owned by the Hebrew Union College (Cincinnati), Jewish Institute of Religion (New York), New York Public Library, Pierpont Morgan Library (New York), Princeton University Library. In England there are magnificent collections in the British Museum, the Bodleian Library at Oxford, and the University Library at Cambridge.

Notwithstanding the great number of MSS. extant (but see p. 191 f.), changes in the formal style of the Hebrew characters between the ninth century (i.e., the date of our earliest pre-served Biblical codices) and the fifteenth century (when the Biblical codices were first printed) appear to have been relatively slight, and the best authorities differ in their attribution of dates on the handwriting alone. Indeed, in view of the stereotyped character of the text preserved in all extant codices, not so much depends on the precise assignment of dates to these codices, as in the case of Greek or Latin MSS.

DEVELOPMENT OF HEBREW ALPHABET

It has been shown (see p. 135) that in the first centuries of the Christian era the Square Hebrew script became standard-

172

ized. We would again emphasize that basically this is still used for writing the *Torah*-scrolls and for the printing of modern Hebrew. There can be no doubt that practically the same script—though in a more primitive style—was already in use in the early second century C.E. when there was a movement for fixing an authoritative text of the Hebrew Bible. It has been suggested that the name most prominently associated with this movement is that of Rabbi Aqiba b. Joseph, who suffered martyrdom under the Romans in the Bar Kochba War. He was an exegete, a teacher, and a systematizer. As exegete, he developed the science of *midrash* to its extreme limits, and gave proof of extraordinary acumen in the interpretations of the Biblical text. As a teacher he became the dominating influence in *Torah*-study for several generations.

The most important of his disciples was R. Meir, the editor of a *mishnah* which became the basis of the *Mishnah* compiled by Judah ha-Nasi ("the Prince"), that is the codification of the Oral Law, which became the uniform textbook of the laws of Judaism. The Talmud links the names of these two great sages, when it says (*Kiddushin* 72b): "when Akiba died Judah was born", or—in the words of Dr. A. Cohen—"what Akiba started Judah completed." Needless to say, Square Hebrew was the script of the *Mishnah* and of the other Hebrew texts.

In the evolution of the later Hebrew alphabet, three fundamental types of writing can be traced: (1) the Square script, which during its bi-millennial history gradually developed into the neat, well-proportioned formal style and printing-type of modern Hebrew; (2) the cursive literary or book-hands, which were the hands employed by the medieval Jewish savants in Spain, Italy, France and Germany, and in the Levant; and (3) the current hands, in many local varieties, of which the Polish Yiddish form, with some insignificant changes, became the current Hebrew hand of today.

STYLES OF HEBREW SCRIPT (Pl. XI)

These three types are not mutually exclusive. Fundamentally, the old Square script was and has always been a monumental script but, with some slight changes in ancient times, it was also used as a literary hand, as a cursive and as a semi-cursive script. The script of the ritual *Torah*-scrolls (see p. 167ff.) is the more elegant, better proportioned, form of it, and has the letter-decorations *taggîn*. A simpler type was used in

173

the Middle Ages for writing Bible codices and has become the standard printing-type of today.

A history of the Hebrew monumental or lapidary style, in the narrow sense of this term, cannot be attempted, particularly not in a book on the Hebrew alphabet. In point of fact, numerous Hebrew inscriptions have been found in Palestine, Italy, Spain, North Africa, Crimea, in the Levant, and other countries, but we cannot, as yet, speak of a style, or styles, distinct from the formal *Torah*-scroll style (without *taggîn*). The Hispano-Hebrew monumental style is perhaps an exception: see Pl. XVI and XIX. See also Pl. XV.

Pl. XIV is a specimen of an early semi-cursive script.

Pl. XVII–XVIII and XXI–XXV reproduce specimens of formal and cursive Hebrew styles from Jerusalem, Spain, France-Germany and Italy.

The medieval literary-hands, particularly the hand known as Rashi-script, were mainly used for non-Biblical manuscripts or the non-Biblical portions of codices such as Commentaries, and also as printing-type for such books. Indeed, "Rashi writing" is still used for Bible commentaries set alongside the Bible text, which is in Square script, when printing copies of medieval Bible codices.

Finally, in the course of time, the various current hands fell out of use, except for the Polish Yiddish hand, which is now employed as the current hand in Israel and for Hebrew in general (see also p. 186 f.). This current hand and the Hebrew formal style and printing-type are the main types used today. See Pl. XXVI–XXVII.

RABBINIC STYLES

It would not be easy to write a comprehensive history of the Rabbinic scripts. The main difficulties are of two kinds: (1) there is insufficient material to write individual histories for single countries, and because of the relatively great local differences, it would be a mistake to try to write a chronological history and replace lacunas in one country with material from another. (2) The form of each letter was on the whole rather constant, and the slight changes which do occur in the course of time are not of great significance for the general reader. In these circumstances, it is preferable to adopt a geographical classification rather than a chronological treatment.

174

Generally speaking, there are very few ligatures in Hebrew writing; the main reason for this scarcity is probably the passage in the Talmud (*Menaḥoth* 29*a*), according to which in the *Mezuzôth* any letter "which is not surrounded on all its four sides by *gewîl* (= parchment)" is not admitted. However, there was one significant exception. The ligature '*aleph–lamed* appears in formal writing in numerous Biblical codices, as well as in Rabbinic and cursive scripts. Also *he*, *waw*, and *yodh* are occasionally joined to the preceding or the following letter, and *mem* and '*ayin* appear in ligatures with the following letter.

MAIN CLASSIFICATION OF CODICES

The preserved Hebrew codices fall into four main families: the Eastern, the Hispano–Portuguese, the Italian, and the Franco-German. The distinction is based upon external and internal criteria.

The main external criteria are:

(*a*) the script, which will be dealt with further on;

(*b*) the writing material: with the exception of the Eastern codices, frequently written on Oriental paper, hardly any Hebrew Biblical codices are written on paper. From the fifteenth century onwards, the Italian Hebrew codices were written on superfine vellum, and the Spanish and Portuguese codices were also written on fine and flexible vellum, whereas this is seldom the case with the Franco-German codices;

(*c*) the format: the Franco-German codices were generally of large size, the Spanish–Portuguese mainly of medium size, and the Italian codices of small size.

Internal criteria:

(*a*) Eastern codices are often written on pages containing only one column; with the exception of some earlier MSS., this is seldom the case with codices belonging to the three other main families; numerous Franco-German codices have three columns to the page, whereas the majority of the Hispano-Portuguese and the Italian codices have two columns to the page;

(*b*) unlike the codices of the other families, the Franco-

175

German show a certain amount of divergence from the Massoretic text, and follow the order of the Biblical books as given in the Talmud.

LOCAL STYLES OF HEBREW SCRIPT

It is, thus, evident that whilst the script is the main external criterion for the geographical, and we may say, partly at least, for the chronological attribution of a codex, it is supplemented by several other criteria. These other criteria are of paramount importance, because it enables us to supplement our knowledge of the local styles and hands.

On the whole, it may be said that the identification of the Franco-German hands, characterized as they are by comparatively rude and inelegant features, is relatively easy. Hebrew Eastern styles, particularly the Maghribi (= "Western", *sc.* from the Oriental viewpoint) and the Yemenite, have a style of their own. The same thing may be said of several Rabbinic and current hands of the Hebrew script in Italy.

On the other hand, it is far from easy to distinguish for the earlier period the Italian formal Hebrew types from the Spanish, or the Spanish and the Provençal Hebrew current hands from Eastern hands, which are transitional from the Rabbinic to the current style. In these and many other instances, because of the dearth of material, judgment must be reserved, unless there are some other valid criteria which can assist in the attribution of the MS. in question.

It is to be borne in mind, too, that local Hebrew scripts were strongly influenced in style by the non-Jewish script and art of their region; as a result, there appear the elegant forms of the Italian Hebrew hands; and, owing to Hispano-Arabic influence, the Spanish and Portuguese Hebrew codices are written in elegantly-formed letters.

The Alphabet-table on Plate XI, will show the reader the relatively insignificant development of the formal, the Rabbinic, and the current hands.

176

CHAPTER 5

MODERN HEBREW ALPHABET AND ADAPTATION TO OTHER TONGUES

As ALREADY STATED, the modern Hebrew alphabet consists of twenty-two letters, all of them consonants, though some have a kind of vocalic power. On the whole, it is fuller than the English alphabet; although it lacks a symbol for *x*—which represents the sounds *ks*—it has a variety of sibilants, gutturals, dentals, and other symbols, which in English have no real equivalents. The characters are written and read from right to left, so that the pages and lines of a Hebrew book begin on the right hand. Many of the letters open towards the left. All the characters are written separately, and as a rule (but see p. 175) are not joined to the preceding or following letter, though current writing presents some exceptions to this rule.

SINGLE-FORM SCRIPT

There is no distinction between majuscules and minuscules (capitals and small letters), the form being the same at the beginning as in the middle of a word. Five letters, however, take a special form when at the end of a word and are called "final" (see also p. 136). These five letters (*k, m, n, p, ṣ*) were combined by Jewish Grammarians in the mnemonic word *kamnèpheṣ* or *ka-menapéṣ*, "as the breaker in pieces". Another mnemonic device—which, however, disregards the alphabetical order—appears in the Talmud, and it is *min-ṣophkha* "of thy watcher" (= "prophet"); some scholars would read *min-ṣophayikh* = "from thy watchmen" (= "prophets"): see *Isaiah*, lii. 8.

Of these letters, the final *mem* is completely closed while the common *mem* is left open and is rounder; the other final letters are distinguished from their more ordinary form by the shaft being drawn straight down instead of bent round towards the left.

Nearly all the letters are of uniform length. The exceptions

177

are the letters *yodh, lamedh, kaph*, and the final letters except *mem*; *yodh* is only half the usual length; *lamedh* rises above, whereas *qoph* and the final letters (except *mem*) descend below the average level of the letters. Six letters have only half the general breadth; these are *gimel, waw, zayin, yodh, nun*, and *'ayin*.

On p. 167 ff. it was said that in sacred writing a word must not be cut short at the end of a line to be completed in the next. In order that no empty space may be left, in MSS. and printed Biblical and other books, certain letters suitable for the purpose are dilated at the end or in the middle of the line (such letters are known as *literae dilatabiles*). This is done mainly with the following five letters: *'aleph, he, lamed, mem, taw*, which are known as the mnemonic device *'ahaltèm*. Sometimes, also, though rather rarely, *daleth, kaph*, and *resh* are used as *literae dilatabiles*.

DIACRITICAL POINTS

Diacritical points have been discussed on p. 151 ff. and will also be referred to on p. 183 ff. Here we have to re-examine the two forms of *dagesh* (see p. 160 f.). The *dagesh lene* is placed in six consonants, the weak and middle-hard palatals, dentals and labials *beth, gimel, daleth, kaph, pe*, and *taw*, which are known mnemonically as the letters $b^e g^a dh \ k^e ph^a th$. These letters are pronounced hard (which was probably the original pronunciation) when the letters contain the dot (as *b, g, d, k, p, t*) and pronounced weak, as "aspirants", without a dot (*bh, gh, dh*, etc.). Our classification of these letters as "aspirants", which is the customary one, is not quite satisfactory, because b^h and k^h are rather *v* and *kh* (Scottish *ch*) than aspirants *bh* and *kh*.

Occasionally, the absence of the *dagesh* in the *begadh-kephath* letters is denoted by a *raphè* (meaning "weak", "soft"), that is a horizontal stroke over the consonant; this is the opposite of *dagesh* and *mappîq* (see below), and particularly of *dagesh lene*.

The *dagesh forte* may be inserted in any letter except the gutturals (*'aleph, he, ḥeth, 'ayin*) and the *resh*, which are known mnemonically as *ha-aḥ rea'* ("the brother friend"). The *dagesh forte*—as said above—doubles the letter, and in the letters *begadh kephath* it doubles and hardens them.

NUMERICAL NOTATION

The Hebrew letters are also used as numerical signs; this usage is not Biblical, and it may have been in imitation of the Greek custom; at any rate, the first traces of it are found on Maccabaean coins (see p. 88 ff.). The letters from *'aleph* to *teth* stand for the units in succession; similarly *yodh* to *sade* for the tens, and *qoph* to *taw* for hundreds (to 400); 500 to 900 are generally expressed by the combination of *taw* with the other signs for hundreds, or, occasionally, by the final letters *kaph* (500), *mem* (600), *nun* (700), *pe* (800), *sade* (900). Two dots over a letter indicate a thousand. Compounds of numbers —thousands, hundreds, tens, and units—are expressed by a combination of letters, those denoting the higher numbers being placed towards the right.

In an indication of the date, the letter indicating the thousands is generally omitted; the numbers "fifteen" and "sixteen" are not denoted by *yodh-he* and *yodh-waw* (since these combinations represent the abbreviated forms of the *Tetragammaton*—see p. 82 f.); the combinations *teth-waw* (9 and 6) and *teth-zayin* (9 and 7) are used instead.

FORM OF LETTERS

On the following page is a table of all the Hebrew letters, their forms, names, phonetic values, and numerical values.

PRONUNCIATION

For their pronunciation these letters can be classified in the following groups:

(*a*) Laryngals or gutturals: *'aleph, he, heth, 'ayin* (being pronounced on the throat).

(*b*) Palatals: *gimel, yodh, kaph, qoph, resh* (pronounced on the palate).

(*c*) Linguals (including partly dentals and sonants): *daleth, teth, lamedh, nun, taw* (pronounced on the tongue).

(*d*) Dentals–sibilants: *zayin, samekh, sade, shin* (*sin*) (pronounced on the teeth).

(*e*) Labials (including partly sonants): *beth, waw, mem, pe* (pronounced on the lips).

179

MODERN HEBREW ALPHABET

Form of Letter				Name	Phonetic Value	N. value
Initial & Medial		Final				
Print	Current	Print	Current			
א	ıc			'aleph	slight breathing with which a vowel is uttered at the beginning of a word; it is, however, a consonant analogous to the silent h (i.e. in 'hour')	1
נ(ב)	(ף) ב			beth (bheth)	b (v)	2
	ג			gimel (ghimel)	g (gh)	3
	ד			daleth	d (dh)	4
	ה			he	h	5
	ו			waw	w (also v)	6
	ז			zayin	3	7
ח	ח			heth	h (or Scotch ch)	8
ט	ט			teth	t (produced by pressing the tongue strongly against the palate	9
	י			yodh	y	10
כ(ב)	(כ) כ	ך	ך	kaph (khaph)	k (kh)	20
	ל			lamedh	l	30
	מ	ם	ם	mem	m	40
	נ	ן	ן	nun	n	50
	ס			samekh	s	60
ע	ע			ayin	rough breathing produced at the back of the throat	70
פ(ב)	(פ) פ	ף	ף	pe (phe)	p (ph)	80
צ	צ	ץ	ץ	sade	s or ts, a sort of hissing s	90
ק	ק			qoph	q pronounced like a strong k formed at the back of the palate	100
ר	ר			resh	r mainly pronounced as palatal with a vibrating uvula	200
ש	ש			shin (sin)	sh or s	300
ת	ת			taw (thaw)	t (th)	400

180

A.C. Sylvester

It must be borne in mind that the pronunciation of Hebrew is not uniform; indeed, there are several forms of pronunciation, including two main ones: *Sephardi*—i.e., that of the "Spanish" (and Portuguese) Jews, also used in the Reform and Liberal Synagogues; and *Ashkenazi* (or "German")—which is the pronunciation of German and East-European Jews; this form is also employed in the reading of the Sacred Scriptures by the majority of the Jewish communities in England and America (their members being almost exclusively of East- or Central-European origin).

R. Loewe has recently shown in *The Mediaeval Christian Hebraists of England*, "Hebrew Union College Annual", 1957, that transliterations of Hebrew into Latin character in English thirteenth-century MSS. imply, broadly speaking, a Sephardi pronunciation rather than the Ashkenazi pronunciation of the Jewries of North France and Germany, "to whose cultural orbit the Jews of mediaeval England belonged". He adds, however, "But the suggestion that a Sephardic type of pronunciation was originally to be found also in France and Germany has now won considerable acceptance; the Tiberian pronunciation was, apparently, being introduced there in the time of Rashi (*ob.* 1105)." See also p. 183.

Interesting instances, partly deviations both from the Sephardi and the Ashkenazi pronunciations are: *b(h)eth* is transliterated *b* or *u* (= *v* or *w*), *d(h)aleth* = *th(orn)*, *ḥeth* is transliterated *h* or omitted, *ṭeth* = *t*, *yodh* = *g*, *kaph* = *c* or *ch*, *samekh* = *s* or *ch*, *p(h)* e = *p* or *f*, *ṣade* = *s* or *c*, *qoph* = *k*, *shin* = *s* or *sh* or *ch*, *t(h)aw* = *t* or *th* or *thz* or *z* or *ch*.

The Sephardi pronunciation has been adopted for modern Hebrew, which has become the official language of the re-born State of Israel, and is also used in modern learned publications, in the press, and so forth, all over the World. The pronunciation of Hebrew by Christians mainly follows the Sephardi pronunciation (at least in the majority of cases); it was introduced in the sixteenth century by the famous German humanist Johannes Reuchlin (1455–1522).

Akin to the Sephardi is the pronunciation of the Jews who follow the Italian rite (which, however, has certain distinctive features as, for instance, *'ayin* being pronounced *gnayin*); and the pronunciation of the Oriental Jews, including the Yemenites (whose distinct pronunciation of *ḥeth, ṭeth, ʿayin, ṣade,* and *qoph* is particularly noteworthy). The Ashkenazi pronunciation itself is far from uniform; for instance, the pronunciation of the German Jews differs considerably from that of the Polish Jews and from that of the Russian Jews; the pronunciation of the English Ashkenazi communities (which is not uniform either), being derived mainly from that of the German Jews has some features of the pronunciation of Russian or Polish Jews.

Amongst the main differences between the Sephardi pronunciation and the Ashkenazi are (1) those relating to accent— in Sephardi this is mainly on the last syllable; in Ashkenazi, mainly on the last but one; and (2) pronunciation of the long vowels, which will be referred to further on.

Moreover, the difference in pronunciation between *ʾaleph* and *ʿayin, ḥeth* and *khaph, ṭeth* and *taw, kaph* and *qoph,* while non-existent in the Ashkenazi pronunciation, is clear in the Sephardi, and particularly so in the Yemenite and other Oriental pronunciations. There is also a clear distinction between Sephardi and Ashkenazi in the pronunciation of the *begadh–kephath* letters (see pp. 160ff. and 178); in the Ashkenazi pronunciation the *dagesh* makes no difference in the pronunciation of *gimel* and *daleth,* and the letters *beth, kaph, pe* and *taw* without the *dagesh* are simply pronounced *v, kh, f* and *s,* respectively.

Of the various Sephardi pronunciations we refer particularly to the Anglo-Sephardi, also current in some American communities. Its main features according to A. D. Corré are: the pronunciation of *beth* and *b(h)eth* as *b; taw* and *t(h)aw,* as well as *ṭeth,* as *t;* on the other hand, *kaph* and *qoph* = *k,* and *k(h)aph* and *ḥeth* = *ch* (as in "loch"). Also *pe* is pronounced *p* and *p(h)e* = *f; ʿayin* (see Italian Hebrew) is pronounced *ng,* while *waw* is not pronounced *w* but *v.* Vocalic marks: *pathaḥ* is pronounced *a* (as in "bar"); *qameṣ* = *a* or *o* according to position; *ṣerê* and *seghôl* = *e* (as in "let"); *ḥireq* = *i* (as in "sieve"); *ḥolêm* = long *o; shûreq* and *qibbûṣ* = *u* (pronounced *oo*); finally *shewâ* is either silent or short *e.*

THEIR ORIGIN

The origin of the division of Hebrew pronunciation into Sephardi and Ashkenazi is not entirely clear. In Prof. Max Weinreich's opinion, the modern Ashkenazi pronunciation is

182

essentially a replica of that of the Northwestern region (see p. 155 f.), while the Sephardi does not deviate much from what was ascribed to the Southwestern region.

The Ashkenazi adherence to the Tiberian pronunciation was, according to Weinreich, relatively late, dating from the thirteenth century C.E. onwards, whereas before that period the speakers of Early Yiddish (see p. 186 f.) used the Palestinian Hebrew pronunciation. Curiously enough—here we quote Prof. Weinreich: "it was the Babylonian teachers, coached in the Tiberias pronunciation and believing in its superiority over all rival reading systems, who are most likely to have steeped their new charges in the imported orthoëpy. They were the carriers of authority concerning the sacred text of the Torah, so there was no doubt that they also knew better than anybody else how to read it." Thus, in Weinreich's opinion, the Ashkenazi pronunciation of Hebrew, through the intervention of the great Jewish scholars from the Talmudic schools of Babylonia—who reached Central Europe by way of Byzantium and the Slavonic countries—became, as we may say, "Tiberianized".

On the other hand—Prof. Weinreich argues—the Sephardi grammarians led by the Qimḥis, particularly David who, though born in Narbonne (in 1160; he also died there, in 1235), belonged to a family hailing from Southern Spain, accepted the Tiberian punctuation but not the pronunciation; they, however, reinterpreted the Tiberian vocalization system as distinguishing between long and short vowels. This "lip service to a writing system", writes Weinreich, "that was so clearly unsuited for the actual pronunciation of the region has been haunting the students of Hebrew grammar ever since". Be this as it may, the whole problem is still *sub judice*.

It is thus uncertain which of the two main pronunciations is the more "correct"; the Sephardi is more closely related to the pronunciation of some kindred Arabic dialects, which have been in long, uninterrupted use; whereas the Ashkenazi partly resembles the Syriac (i.e., late Aramaic) pronunciation, which was also in uninterrupted use.

MODERN VOCALIC REPRESENTATION

In modern Hebrew vocalized texts as many as fourteen vocalic sounds can be expressed by diacritic points. Each

183

mark has a name, which generally indicates the nature of the sound or the movement of the organ of speech employed to produce it. The names are (see also p. 157):

pathah, "opening" (the sound produced with the open mouth);

seghôl, by exception named after the form of the sign, "bunch of grapes";

hireq (or *hireq qaton*, "little" or short *hireq*), "narrow opening"; "gnashing";

qibbuṣ, "compression" or firmer contraction of the mouth;

qameṣ denotes a "slighter compression" of the mouth;

ṣerê means "dividing", a wide parting of the lips;

shûreq (see below), "whistling";

holêm, "fullness" or "closing" (of the mouth);

there is also *hireq gadhôl*, "great" or long *hirêq*;

qameṣ haṭuph, "rapid compression".

Most of these vowel-marks are placed below the consonant; *holêm* is a dot placed above the letter. Several of the long vowels are associated with one of the following letters: *'aleph, he, waw, yodh*; *shûreq* and full *holem*, indeed, consist of the letter *waw* with a dot inside, in the former case, or above it, in the latter. The *hireq gadhôl* and *ṣerê* are often associated with a *yodh* following the vocalized consonant, whereas consonants vocalized with the long vowels *seghôl* and *qameṣ* may be followed by an *'aleph* or a *he*; the *seghôl* also by a *yodh*.

In all, there are five short-vowel marks:

pathah, for the sound *a* (as in "anti"); [-]

seghôl, for the sound *e* (as in "let"); [⸪]

hireq qaṭôn, or short *hireq*, for the sound *i* (as the *i* in "sieve"); [·]

qibbûṣ, for the sound *u* (as in "full"); [⸪]

and *qameṣ haṭûph*, for the sound *o* (as in "not"). [⸕⸳]

The six long-vowel marks are:

qameṣ, for the sound *a* (as in "father") or, in Ashkenazi pronunciation, *u* (as in "rule"); [⸕]

ṣerê, for the sound *ai* (as in "pain") or *e* (as in "they"), or else, in Ashkenazi, *ai* (as *i* in "line"); [··]

long *hîreq*, for the *i* (as in "machine"); [⸳·]

hôlem, for the sound *o* (as in "holy") or, in Ashkenazi, *oi* (as in "ointment"); [⸗]

184

shûreq, represented by a *waw* with a dot inside, for the sound *u* (as in "goose"), or—in Ashkenazi—a sound similar to *i* in "lid", but long; [‎ו]
qibbuṣ may sometimes be employed for a long vowel with a sound similar to that of *shûreq*.

Apart from these full-vowel marks, there are marks for semi-vowels, indistinct vowel-sounds, "silent" vowels. To these belongs first of all the *shewâ*, generally a most indistinct sound resembling the swift *e* in "the". It may be "simple" or "composite". In the former case, it may be "vocal" or "mobile"— this occurs when it is placed under the first consonant of a word or a syllable, and it represents a very short *e* as the first *e* in "believe" (in Ashkenazi pronunciation it is silent). A *shewâ* which is placed under a consonant which closes a syllable is silent, and is called *shewâ quiescens*; it may be regarded as a simple syllable divider; there is also a poor half and half thing known as *medial shewâ* or *shewâ medium*.

The other three indistinct vowel-marks (the composite-*shewâ* marks) approach so much towards distinctness that the class of vowel-sound to which they belonged can be detected; they practically reached the stage of the vowel, but stopped on the threshold. These three marks are known as *ḥaṭeph* ("hurried") signs; they are made up, or compounded, of a simple *shewâ* and a short vowel, this being written to the left of the *shewâ*.

There are three *ḥaṭephs*: *ḥaṭeph-pathaḥ*, *ḥaṭeph-seghôl*, and *ḥaṭeph-qameṣ*; they are chiefly used (*ḥaṭeph-seghôl* exclusively so) to vocalize gutturals—*'aleph*, *he*, *ḥeth*, *'ayin*—because a simple *shewâ* is insufficient to secure the distinct pronunciation of such letters.

As already mentioned, vowel-marks nowadays are used only in printed Bibles, text-books for schools, prayer-books, poetry, and similar matter where there is risk of confusion.

OTHER TONGUES WRITTEN WITH HEBREW CHARACTERS
Pl. XXVI

In this connection, a main principle and a general problem might be considered. The main principle—already referred to on p. 43—is *Alphabet follows Religion*. That the Alphabet

185

follows Trade or the Flag is a general belief, based on experience of the last centuries; it is partly true. Earlier times, however, gave striking examples of the proposition that the Alphabet follows Religion. This dictum was true for all the main religions: Zoroastrianism, Judaism, Christianity, Islam, Buddhism, Manichaeism.

It is particularly applicable to the Square Hebrew script. Following the migration of Jews and of a Jewish sect (the Karaites, who adopted the language of their new countries though continuing to use Hebrew as their liturgical language) the Hebrew script was adapted to several languages, some belonging to quite different linguistic families. It was used to write Arabic, which like Hebrew is a Semitic language, but also to write Turkish (as originally employed by the Karaites in the Crimea), Persian or Iranian, early French, Italian, and particularly German and Spanish. The script was also adopted for Judaeo-German or Yiddish, and Judaeo-Spanish or Judezmo, also called Ladino.

ADAPTATION OF THE HEBREW ALPHABET

The general problem, to which we must now turn, is the adaptation of a script to a new language, especially when that form of speech belongs to another linguistic family and contains sounds not found in the speech from which the alphabet has been adapted. There is the difficulty of representing the new sounds, a difficulty which is solved in different ways.

In the case of the Hebrew alphabet there is, needless to say, the additional difficulty that a script without vowels could hardly serve, for instance, an Indo-European language such as German or Spanish. The main procedure adopted was that of taking over the *matres lectionis* (see p. 151 f.) as pure vowels and enlarging their use.

The same device was used for the transliteration of foreign proper names. But the device is not uniform and is not used for the transcription of words borrowed from Hebrew which maintain their original orthography; so, for instance, the Yiddish word *emes*, "truth, true", is written as in Hebrew without vowels, *'mt*, though in Soviet Russia in recent times Hebrew words are also written "phonetically".

Wherever the Hebrew alphabet was adopted for, and adapted to other languages, the direction of Hebrew writing, from right to left, was retained. As far as is practicable, the

186

spelling is phonetic, though not scientifically so. Space does not permit of detailed analysis, which in any case would take us beyond the aims of the present work. We may, however, mention that in Yiddish the letters *'aleph, waw, yodh* and *'ayin* respectively, are used as the vowels *a* or *o, u, i* (*y*) and *e*; double *yodh* represents the diphthongs *ei* or *ai*, while the diphthong *oi* is represented by the combination *waw-yodh*.

This vowel-representation is by no means uniform, particularly as the pronunciation of Yiddish differs from dialect to dialect. Dr. J. Maitlis, who has recently published some London Dutch-Yiddish letters of the early eighteenth century, has pointed out that in Dutch Yiddish we may notice the characteristic mark of Western Yiddish whereby the medieval German diphthongs *ai, ou,* and *öü* became *aa.* So for instance Western Yiddish *Frand, kafen, natik* correspond with Eastern Yiddish *Freind, koifen, naitik,* etc.

CONCLUSION

IS A REFORM OF THE HEBREW ALPHABET NECESSARY OR PRACTICABLE?

IT IS UNQUESTIONABLE that the Hebrew Alphabet is extremely complicated, particularly for non-specialists who desire to master Hebrew as they can master any Western language. One may even wonder whether leading experts who have advocated the reform of the Hebrew alphabet, have themselves realized how intricate the Hebrew script is if we consider the whole problem, including vowel marks, and other diacritic points.

Indeed, when a leading artist in typography, Stanley Morison, approves the suggestion that "the Jewish community, while retaining the old hieratic signs for its liturgies, needs to choose for its newspapers and its ephemeric an alphabet of Roman equivalents for Hebrew sounds, or . . . a Romanized Hebrew", he refers merely to the idea of a technical, typographical reform of the Hebrew consonantal letters, without, it appears, giving thought to the complicated little marks to be placed above, below, to the right, to the left and inside these letters. And it is a good thing that Mr. Morison has overlooked the main problem; otherwise, he would not have thought that reform was as easy as he suggested, and we should probably have been deprived of his valuable contribution.

SINGLE-FORM SCRIPT IMPEDES TYPOGRAPHICAL DEVELOPMENT

No lover of beautiful type would disagree with Stanley Morison, when he writes: "Unbending conservatism has achieved no typographical result more hampering to a community than the forcing of modern Hebrew into the strait-waistcoat of an alphabet five times as ancient as the type of the First Folio. In spite of the fact that the Roman and Greek alphabets . . . developed on interchangeable duplex series of signs, in their capital and lower-case, most apt for the

188

expression of varied emphasis, Hebrew has remained as it was when Nehemiah and Ezra published the Law. The Roman alphabet has developed, in its italic, a still more effective means of assisting the reader's instant understanding of distinctive parts of one harmonious setting. In full sight of these developments the Jews have maintained until today their original single-form alphabet of square 'capitals' . . . that a world-people should have preserved the jot and tittle of a script for two and a half millenniums is a remarkable phenomenon—a triumph, it must be allowed, for the conservative spirit, yet by no means a satisfaction of the purpose for which the alphabet is needed today, namely, the service of a community whose transactions have been expanded to infinity by the printing press." This was written over a quarter of a century ago, and today, need it be said, these words possess far greater pungency.

The authority from whom we have just quoted, wrote an excellent *Introduction* to an original effort of reform of the Hebrew printing type by an enthusiastic lover of artistic print, Hugh J. Schonfield (*The New Hebrew Typography*, London, Denis Archer, 1932). Reforms of the Hebrew alphabet have been suggested before. It will suffice to refer to the movement for the adoption of the Latin alphabet, with supporters of high standing such as the late nationalist leader Vladimir Jabotinsky. Such radical reforms, it is felt, have no chance of success.

INADEQUACIES OF PRESENT HEBREW TYPOGRAPHY

Mr. Schonfield points out the following defects in the present Hebrew typography: (*a*) Hebrew characters are of one order; they have no distinct capital letters and lower-case (i.e. small) letters. Values, cannot, therefore, be differentiated. (*b*) The squareness retards flow. (*c*) The color is on the black side in horizontal bands; so that it does not match with Western type which is vertical in weight. (*d*) There is an absence of expression, making it impossible to select a Hebrew type for its appropriateness to the subject matter. "Collectively" —writes Mr. Schonfield—"these deficiencies debar Hebrew from universal service." Nowadays, of course, several excellent new type-faces exist in Israel and in the U.S.A. See also p. 193.

189

What remedies does Hugh Schonfield suggest? He has created an ingenious alphabet consisting of characters, which in his opinion "are perfectly good Hebrew, and perhaps, because some of the letters are based on more archaic exemplars, a truer Hebrew than the square characters they are intended to supersede for general purposes". All this being correct, Mr. Schonfield does not tell us that his alphabet is still without vowels, this being the main shortcoming of the current Hebrew alphabet, and that his reform is much too radical to have any chance of acceptance.

In other words, his creation does not try to tackle the main problem, that of the vowels. As to his radicalism, his alphabet is so completely changed that it does not resemble any other script, Hebrew or otherwise. It is, however, based on serious research, the new forms being derived from old ones.

Schonfield explains how he constructed his lower-case letters: his *aleph* is based on the Rabbinic *aleph* (the vertical stroke being bent over to the right). *Beth*, apart from the vertical emphasis, follows the Rabbinic. *Gimel*: slightly adapted from an old Yemenite form; *daleth*: a diminutive of the capital. *He* is based on first-century Hebrew inscriptions with the ascender extend; also *waw* is based on first-century Hebrew inscriptions; *zayin* is inspired by Eastern MS.-cursives; *heth* adapted from the Rabbinic style . . . *Nun* is inspired by Maccabaean coins; *samekh* is Eastern Rabbinic . . . *Pe* is adapted from the final form of this letter; . . . *qoph* is based on pre-exilic seals and inscriptions; *resh* is adapted from early inscriptions; *shin* is a variation of the usual form, obtained by joining the two branches, with emphasis on the vertical curve; and *taw* is created from the Early Hebrew cruciform and the Square character. "It thus presents the onomatopoeic form of 'th' reversed."

As to the capitals, Mr. Schonfield explains, he has adopted the present Hebrew characters, and in his opinion, "with a few minor alterations and, of course, the serifs and vertical emphasis, they will be found to agree with the traditional forms". Be this as it may, even his capital letters do not look as if they are Hebrew.

In short, while I agree that the forms Mr. Schonfield has created "are harmonious even to the careful distribution of ascenders and descenders" and that he has "demonstrated that a modern Hebrew Typography is practicable", I do not think that the principles on which he has worked "will be shown to be sound ones".

PURELY TYPOGRAPHICAL REFORM NECESSARY AND PRACTICABLE

A reform of the Hebrew alphabet is overdue, but it must not deprive modern Jews of a link with their multi-millennial history. Indeed, the ancient Semitic creative impetus, the colorful ingenious reforms of the learned Jewish grammarians of the early Middle Ages, the millennial struggle for religious and national survival are reflected in the Hebrew alphabet. A reform which pays due regard to these and other historical circumstances may have a chance of success.

If I had to suggest a complete reform, I would favor a return to the Early Hebrew alphabet, the script of the Hebrew kings and prophets, a script which in its various styles and in the distinctiveness of its letters could easily be pressed into modern service. But I do realize that it would be very difficult to do away with the conditions produced by the Jewish history over the last two thousand years.

Here it may not be out of place to point out a few facts of the tragic history of the Jewish people and the Hebrew book. Poignantly we may also refer to some *general* remarks of a great book-lover, H. Jackson. "The trials and tribulation of books," wrote Jackson, "are equalled only by the trials and tribulations of mankind; their sufferings are identical with those of their creators, and if they live longer they are not immune from decay and death. They have been beaten and burnt, drowned, tortured, imprisoned, suppressed, executed, censored, exiled, reviled, condemned, buried; they are over-worked and underworked, misused and maltreated in every manner known to fate and chance and the most ingenious of miscreants and misguided zealots."

Hebrew literary production over the past three thousand years has been very vast—traditionally the Jews are called *'am ha-sepher*, "The People of the Book"—but only a very small portion of this literature has survived. It is not difficult to indicate the main reasons for this fact. As early as the time of the persecution of Antiochus Epiphanes (175–164 B.C.E.) there is a pointer: see 1 *Macc.* i. 56 f.

Later, throughout the long centuries of the darkness which closed in upon the Jews after the loss of their independence, the clouds of prejudice and of persecution hung low and lowering over all the countries in which Jews dwelt, and various inquisitions and all kinds of censorships, the burning of books, and so on, repeatedly attempted to eradicate Hebrew literature altogether.

One of the most striking facts in the general history of beautiful book-production is the sudden re-emergence of France about the beginning of the thirteenth century, from comparative obscurity, and her rapid advance to the leading position in book-illumination which she occupied from the time of St. Louis (1226–70) until the middle of the fifteenth century. At the same time, however, in Paris (in June, 1242) twenty-four cartloads of Hebrew manuscripts were publicly burnt, and similar destruction occurred in various other places.

The Renaissance opened men's eyes and minds so that they could both see and comprehend the meaning of what they saw. By creating a demand for books, Renaissance made printing inevitable. From Mainz where a considerable volume of printing was done in the 1450's, the art of printing spread quickly throughout Europe. By 1487 there were printing establishments from Sweden to Portugal. But, in the same period, in 1478, Ferdinand and Isabella, upon permission of the Pope, established the Spanish Inquisition, which was also extended to the Netherlands, and some decades later the Roman Inquisition, or Holy Office, founded in 1542, was active in Italy.

Is it to be wondered at, that the Jewish genius in the realm of the study of the Bible and of defense of Judaism against the hostility of the surrounding World had no counterpart in the realm of artistic printing?

Unfortunately, however, even in recent times, notwithstanding the general improvement of the Jewish situation, Hebrew printing had no William Morris or Cobden-Sanderson, no Eric Gill or J. van Krimpen or Rudolph Koch or Stanley Morison.

PRACTICAL REMEDIES

It is to be noted that none of the creators of the new typefaces changed the forms of the Latin letters; they merely produced more regular and artistic styles of the same letter-

192

forms. A wise regularizing and refinement of the Hebrew type-faces, based on traditional forms, but modified to suit modern production methods, is overdue and practicable. The Hebrew printing trade should train its craftsmen to higher standards of design and technology; Hebrew education authorities, in Israel and the Diaspora, should become aware of the importance and need of higher standards of design and workmanship in the craft; the more educated sections of the public should become conscious that there are standards in the realm of type design. A select committee of highly skilled letter designers, type-founders, and printers, and other enthusiastic experts might be able to produce beautiful Hebrew type-faces in keeping with modern demands and advances.

To be sure, the last twenty-five years have seen the production of better type-faces, which were tidied up and set to work in modern surroundings—it will suffice to refer, for instance, to the 1956 Winter Exhibition in New York's Jewish Museum, with examples of Bible typography by leading contemporary book designers and the ornamental use of Hebrew script by Ludwig Wolpert, a Jewish German artist who emigrated to Palestine in 1933—but the picture is far from perfect; even the best standards of design now available are not as high as is practically possible, and many designs are produced today which are correspondingly bad; some newspapers and magazines are among the worst offenders.

I come back to Stanley Morison; he writes: "The fact is that the Jew *qua* Jew has not yet come of age typographically— his position is analogous with that of Adolph Rusch of Strassburg who, *circa* 1463, was faced with the decision whether or not to adopt the first of all Roman types. It is time that the Jew became a whole-hearted printer."

He is right; he is also right when he says: "Just as the Roman letter which we now use is not a written thing, but an engraved thing, Hebrew script must be transformed by the hand and tool of the engraver. If this had been done, let us say, by Gerson Soncino, in association with the creator of the finest Roman fount of all time, Francesco Griffo, Hebrew typography might long ago have been comparable with Roman."

Gerson Soncino lived at a time when Jews had other and more serious problems to contend with, but today Mr. Morison's advice is practicable. The question, as he writes, "is

193

BIBLIOGRAPHY

THE SUBJECT AS a whole has hardly been dealt with extensively in any single work. Books dealing with the history of the Alphabet in general, have also sections treating of the Hebrew alphabet. Articles on the Hebrew alphabet and palaeography will be found in all Jewish Encyclopaedias. There is, however, a vast literature on the detailed problems examined in this book; this is quoted in D. Diringer, *The Alphabet*, London and New York, 4th Impression, 1953; and *The Hand-Produced Book*, London and New York, 1953. Hebrew Palaeography has been dealt with by C. Bernheimer, *Paleografia ebraica*, Florence, 1924. A new work on *Hebrew Palaeography*, by Dr. S. Birnbaum, is in course of publication; three fascicles have already appeared. Numerous problems regarding the Yiddish language and its (Hebrew) script are worthily dealt with by U. Weinrich and others, *The Field of Yiddish*, etc., New York, 1954 (with copious bibliography also on the Hebrew script).

Scientific Hebrew Grammars (we may refer, for instance, to Prof. J. Weingreen's *Hebrew Grammar*) generally contain sections on the Hebrew alphabet, its consonants, the vowel-marks, the *dagesh*, accents, and so on.

492.411
D59